On the True Philosopher
and the True Philosophy—Essays
on Swedenborg

On the True Philosopher and the True Philosophy—Essays on Swedenborg

Edited by
Stephen McNeilly

Journal of the Swedenborg Society
Swedenborg House
20-21 Bloomsbury Way
London WC1A 2TH

—

2003

ACKNOWLEDGEMENTS

Special thanks to Daniel Cartwright, Heather Ferguson, Emma Keast and Lara Muth for their suggestions and close reading of the texts. Thanks are also extended to Clifford Marcus and Ute Decker - Interpreting & Translation Services for the translation of the articles *Representation and Concept in Swedenborg* by José Antonio Antón-Pacheco and *Swedenborg Biology and Metaphysics* by Francesca Maria Crasta.
The paper by Lars Bergquist titled *Swedenborg and Heavenly Hermeneutics*, although delivered as a lecture at the Swedenborg Society in 1994, was first published in *Arcana* by the Swedenborg Association. It is published here by kind permission of the author.

Volume Two of the 'Journal of the Swedenborg Society'

Enquiries concerning guidelines
for submission, editorial policy and information on future editions
should be directed to the Editor at the address below.

Editor: Stephen McNeilly
Assistant-to-the-Editor: Paul McNeilly

Published by:
The Swedenborg Society
Swedenborg House
20-21 Bloomsbury Way
London WC1A 2TH

© First published 2002. The Swedenborg Society

Book Design and Artwork: Stephen McNeilly
Typeset at Swedenborg House.
Printed and bound in Great Britain
at Biddles.

ISBN 0 85448 134 6
British Library Cataloguing-in-Publication Data.
A Catalogue record for this book is available
from the British Library.

Table of Contents

	Page no.
Notes on Contributors	vii
Chronological list of Works by Swedenborg	ix
Introduction *Stephen McNeilly*	xiii

1—Swedenborg and Kant on Spiritual Intuition *Michelle Grier*..................................1

2—Swedenborg's *Positive* Influence on the Development of Kant's Mature Moral Philosophy *Gregory R Johnson*..................................21

3—Metaphysics and Biology: Thoughts on the Interaction of the Soul and Body in Emanuel Swedenborg *Francesca Maria Crasta*..................................39

4—Swedenborg and the Comparative Philosophy of the Soul *Michael Costello*..................................59

5—Swedenborg and Schopenhauer *Gregory R Johnson*..................................77

6—Swedenborg and Heavenly Hermeneutics *Lars Bergquist*..................................97

7—Representation and Concept in Swedenborg *José Antonio Antón-Pacheco*..................................111

Index..................................125

Contributors

Lars Bergquist is a novelist, essayist and translator, and former Swedish ambassador to China and Italy. Among the many works published in Sweden include *Per brahes undergång och bärgning*, *Isvandring med Nordenskiöld*, and *Den heliga pyramiden*. He has also translated works into Swedish including Chinese Tang poetry and novels by Leonardo Sciascia. His English publications include *Swedenborg's Dream Diary* (Swedenborg Foundation, 2001). He has written a biography of Swedenborg, a translation of which is soon to be published by the Swedenborg Society.

Michael Costello completed his Doctorate in Psychology at the University of Aberdeen in 1981. His philosophical interests include René Descartes, John Locke, David Hume, George Berkeley, C D Broad, G F Stout, C S Pierce, Thomas Reid, William Hamilton and Bertrand Russell, among others. He has also studied zoology. He has been a reader of Swedenborg since 1960.

Francesca Maria Crasta is Associate Professor of the History of Philosophy at the University of Cagliari, Italy. Her initial interests lay in medieval and eighteenth century cosmology, and the spread of Cartesianism in Italy. She has studied anti-Cartesian positions of the eighteenth century in relation to Leibnizian-Wolffian metaphysics. Her publications include *Pianeti e teorie del cielo nel '700* (Torino, 1980); *Swedenborg and Eighteenth Century Cosmology* (New Philosophy no. 3, 1990); *Sulla presenza di Descartes nella 'Galleria di*

Minerva' (Giornale critico della filosofia italiana LXXV, III, 1996); *'Gli effetti son fatti e la ragioni son parole': Scipione Maffei nell'Europa del '700* (Verona, 1998); *La Filosofia della Natura di Emanuel Swedenborg* (Milano, 1999); *Per un'anatomia dell'anima: Emanuel Swedenborg versus Christian Wolff* (Ragione, Natura, Storia Milano, 2000).

Michelle Grier is an Associate Professor of Philosophy at the University of San Diego, California. Her areas of research include Kant, Hegel, History of Modern Philosophy, and Post-Kantian Continental Philosophy. She has published numerous articles on Kant's theoretical philosophy and is the author of *Kant's Doctrine of Transcendental Illusion* (Cambridge University Press, 2001).

Gregory R Johnson is currently Visiting Scholar at the Swedenborgian House of Studies at the Pacific School of Religion in Berkeley, California. He holds a Ph.D. in philosophy from the Catholic University of America in Washington, D.C. His doctoral dissertation, 'A Commentary on Kant's *Dreams of a Spirit-Seer*', argues that Kant adopted central tenets of his mature critical philosophy from Swedenborg. He has published widely on the Kant-Swedenborg relationship and is the translator of Immanuel Kant, *Dreams of a Spirit-Seer and Other Writings on Swedenborg* (Swedenborg Foundation, forthcoming). He has written editorial introductions to Swedenborg's *Divine Love and Wisdom* and *Divine Providence* for the Swedenborg Foundation's New Century Edition of Swedenborg's Writings.

Stephen McNeilly is a Lecturer in Art and Critical Theory at the University of Kent, England. He has previously edited a collection of essays by the noted linguist Dr John Chadwick entitled *On the Translator and the Latin Text* (Swedenborg Society, 2001), and an anthology of contemporary poetry entitled *x24* (Black Dog Press, 1997). He is currently working on a collection of essays to be published in the summer of 2003.

José Antonio Antón Pacheco is Professor of Philosophy at the Universidad de Seville, Spain. He has written on metaphysics, hermeneutics, traditionalist thought and themes connected with Emanuel Swedenborg. He has published numerous articles in Spain including his *Symbolica Nomina: Introducción a la hermenéutica espiritual del Libro*. He is also the author of *Visionary Consciousness: Emanuel Swedenborg and the Immanence of Spiritual Reality* (Arcana Books, 2000).

Selected Works by Swedenborg

Listed chronologically

Published by Swedenborg

1709	Selected Sentences, (*Selectae Sententia*).
1716	Northern Inventor, (*Daedalus Hyperboreus*).
1721	On Finding Longitude, (*Methodus Nova Inveniendi Longitudines Locorum Terra Marique Ope Lunae*).
	Principles of Chemistry, (*Prodromus Principiorum Rerum Naturalium, Sive Novorum Tentaminum Chymian et Physicam*).
	The Principia, Or Principles of Natural Things, (*Principia Rerum Naturalium*).
1734	The Infinite and Final Cause of Creation, (*Prodromus Philosophiae Ratiocinantis de Infinito, et Causa Finali Creationis*).
1740-42	The Economy of the Animal Kingdom, (*Oeconomia Regni Animalis*).
1744	The Animal Kingdom, (*Regnum Animalis*).
1745	The Worship and Love of God, (*De Cultu et Amore Dei*).
1749-1756	Arcana Caelestia, (*Arcana Coelestia*).
1758	Earths in the Universe, (*De Telluribus in Mundo Nostri Solari*).
	Heaven and Hell, (*De Coelo et ejus Mirabilibus, et de Inferno*).
	The Last Judgment, (*De Ultimo Judicio*).
	The New Jerusalem and its Heavenly Doctrine, (*De Nova Hierosolyma*

	et ejus Doctrina Coelesti).
	The White Horse, (*De Equo Albo*).
1763	Doctrine of the New Jerusalem concerning the Lord, (*Doctrina Novae Hierosolymae de Domino*).
	Doctrine of the New Jerusalem concerning the Sacred Scripture, (*Doctrina Novae Hierosolymae de Scriptura Sacra*).
	Doctrine of Life for the New Jerusalem, (*Doctrina Vitae pro Nova Hierosolyma ex Praeceptis Decalogi*).
	Doctrine of the New Jerusalem concerning Faith, (*Doctrina Novae Hierosolymae de Fide*).
	Continuation of The Last Judgment, (*Continuatio de Ultimo Judicio*).
	Divine Love and Wisdom, (*De Divino Amore et de Divina Sapientia*).
1764	Divine Providence, (*De Divina Providentia*).
1766	The Apocalypse Revealed, (*Apocalypsis Revelata*).
1768	Conjugial Love, (*De Amore Conjugiali*).
1769	Brief Exposition, (*Summaria Expositio Doctrinae Novae Ecclesiae*).
	Interaction of the Soul and Body, (*De Commercio Animae et Corporis*).
1771	The True Christian Religion, (*Vera Christiana Religio*).

Published Posthumously

1719	On Tremulation, (*Anatomi af vår aldrafinaste natur, wisande att vårt rörande och lefwande wäsende består af contremiscentier*).
1734	Mechanism of the Soul and Body, (*De Mechanismo Animae et Corporis*).
1738–40	The Cerebrum, (*untitled MS*).
1739	Journeys 1710-1739, (*Itinerarium ex Annis*).
1742	Rational Psychology (or The Soul), (*Psychologia Rationalis*).
	Ontology, (*Ontologia*).
	On Generation, (*De Generatione*).

Chronological List of Works

1743-44	The Brain, (*De Cerebro*).
	The Journal of Dreams, (*Swedenborg's Drömmar*).
	A Philosopher's Notebook, (*untitled MS*).
1744	Hieroglyphic Key, (*Clavis Hieroglyphica*).
	Correspondences and Representations, (*De Correspondentia et Representatione*).
1746-47	The Word Explained, (*Explicatio in Verbum Historicum Veteris Testamenti*).
	Index Biblicus, (*untitled MS*).
1747-1765	The Spiritual Diary, (*Diarium Spirituale*).
1757-1759	The Apocalypse Explained, (*Apocalypsis Explicata*).
1759	Athanasian Creed, (*De Athanasii Symbolo*).
1760	The Lord, (*De Domino*).
1761	Prophets and Psalms, (*Summaria Expositio Sensu Interni Librorum Propheticorum ac Psalmorum*).
	The Sacred Scripture or Word of the Lord, from Experience, (*De Scriptura Sacra seu Verbo Domini*).
1762	Precepts of the Decalogue, (*De Praeceptis Decalogi*).
	The Last Judgment (Posth), (*De Ultimo Judicio*).
	The Divine Love, (*De Divino Amore*).
1763	The Divine Wisdom, (*De Divino Sapientia*).
1766	Conversations with Angels, (*Colloquia cum Angelis*).
	Charity, (*De Charitate*).
	Five Memorable Relations, (*Memorabilia*).
	Marriage, (*De Conjugo*).
1769	Canons of the New Church, (*Canones Novae Ecclesiae*).
	Scripture Confirmations, (*Dicta Probantia*).
	Index to Formula Concordiae, (*Index ad Formulam Concordiae*).
1770	Ecclesiastical History of the New Church, (*Historia Ecclesiatica Novae Ecclesiae*).
1771	Nine Questions, (*Quaestiones Novem de Trinitate*).

On the True Philosopher—Essays on Swedenborg

Reply to Ernesti, (*Responsum ad Dr Ernesti*).
Coronis, (*Coronis seu Appendix ad Veram Christianam Religionem*).
Consummation of the Age and Invitation to the New Church, (*De Consummatione Saeculi, de Adventu Secundo Domini*).
Fragment on Miracles, (*De Miraculis*).

Introduction

Stephen McNeilly

A truth is never absolutely single or simple even though when it is formed it may appear to be so. It is nothing less than a combination of an infinity of other truths, that is, of an infinity of distinct ideas and notions; both a conclusion and a judgment resulting from an orderly disposition of many things. Harmony, as such, can be understood as the unity of particulars and ratios of truth properly co-ordinated (as for example, symbolic or algebraic equations, where a number of terms are conjoined as signs, but are nevertheless represented as single and simple). Such too is the case with all known forms in the universe—because all forms are the result of an infinity of compounds subordinated and combined which can likewise be given attributes, qualities, modes and mutations. Such are truths.[1] —*Swedenborg*

With the possible exception of *The New Philosophy*,[2] few systematic attempts have been made to integrate the work of Emanuel Swedenborg into the history of ideas. Papers have been written pin-pointing an influence on prominent thinkers (e.g. F W J Schelling,[3] Ralph Waldo Emerson,[4] etc.) but little has been done to introduce his thought directly to philosophical debate. Today, when one encounters the name of Swedenborg, one does so primarily as a footnote to specialist studies of the eighteenth century. Even here however, he is misquoted, misjudged or simply misunderstood.

What is the reason for this neglect? In 1766 the philosopher Immanuel Kant published an attack on Swedenborg entitled *Dreams of a Spirit-Seer*.[5] Raising the charge of 'enthusiast' (*schwärmerei*), Kant dismissed Swedenborg as a fanatic. With the subsequent success of Kant's *Critical Philosophy* and the general shift of theoretical studies towards a scientific and rationally grounded discourse, Swedenborg's position became increasingly marginalised. According to Kant for instance, the observation offered by Swedenborg in his *Arcana Caelestia*[6]—that discourse with angels and spirits was possible—rendered his entire method 'critically' unsound, and irrelevant to further philosophic enquiry. This view, in turn, was later evoked by Karl Jaspers as proof of Swedenborg's mental illness.

A closer look at Swedenborg's written output however—rooted as it is in both scientific and esoteric traditions[7]—reveals a more subtle and discerning methodology. For instance, an early central tenet (anticipating Kant's *Critical Project*), states that the initial step of all theoretical enquiry (either theological or philosophical) is to admit that the *esse* of things is unknowable.[8] The aspect of a 'thing' that submits itself to the rational enquiry, he argues, is the manner by which we might assume *esse* to manifest itself. This is what Swedenborg would call its 'truth' or *existere*. Kant himself—and wholly in agreement with Swedenborg here—was later to recast this as the distinction between noumena (the thing-in-itself) and phenomena. One cannot make an appeal to reason in order to elucidate the essence or *esse* of matter, Swedenborg argues. One can only make an appeal to *existere*. The basic structure of such an appeal, in turn, divides into a further twofold distinction.

In the first instance—and revealing surprising parallels to both post-modern and post-structuralist discourses—Swedenborg outlines the initial manifestation of this distinction as a plurality, a network of relations without an orthodox centre. In this sense, he suggests, 'truth' is to be understood as a kind of mutation. Here he uses the analogy of a spider's web and the image of natural philosophy as the spider (the philosopher chooses a position within the 'infinite radii', moving from circle to circle).[9] 'One cannot open one truth', he states, 'without an infinity of others being opened'[10] which consequently derives its context from other truths 'which constitute, form and determine it'.[11] Each truth as such, is never an end in itself but a connection—a link. The more truths that converge, the 'more brilliant and beautiful the light from which these truths are formed'.[12]

In the second instance, and anticipating a certain Nietzschian fervour, such truths are also said to hold correlation to *intensity*. According to Swedenborg, a philosopher is one who *sees*, a witness to intensities and their networks. The occasion of each truth is never itself encountered in isolation (i.e. within every network, there is a 'relation' and within every relation there is guidance). In the same manner, no universal Truth (*aeterna veratis*) is encountered in its totality. Each truth—both singular and universal—is only observable and possible within a realisation of activity (or to quote Swedenborg's later term 'use'). A truth reveals itself when it happens, it is not an *abstraction* detached from the world (for example in the manner of the Truth asserted by dogmatic theology). It is entirely dependent on phenomenon. Neither truth nor phenomena as such, are 'ends' in themselves. It is the manner by which such phenomena display their 'use' or are applied that truth is said to exist—it is the 'use' which determines the 'end'.

One strategy for the papers collected here, therefore, is to explore such nuances in Swedenborg's philosophy. On the one hand this means freeing Swedenborg from the shadow of Kant's attack. On the other hand this means detaching his work from the secondary literature of religious apologists who have seemingly misunderstood the wider implications of his philosophical claims. A further strategy involves placing Swedenborg more clearly within the context of his time and reconsidering the possible significance of his work today.

Articles one and two deal directly with the problem of Kant's attack. Michelle Grier, begins with a detailed reading of Kant's text *Dreams of a Spirit-Seer*, showing Kant to be divided in his response to Swedenborg. On many occasions, she suggests, Kant shows a general sympathy towards a number of Swedenborgian themes, even indicating, at times, a sensitivity to the possibility of Swedenborg's 'spirit reports'.[13] Gregory R Johnson, developing this theme, takes a step further and specifies what he argues as Swedenborg's positive influence on Kant. The example that he draws attention to is Kant's famous attempt to integrate the laws of freedom (i.e. of the subject) with the laws of necessity (i.e. of nature). It is via Swedenborg, Johnson claims, that Kant secured his belief in the distinction between a noumenal and phenomenal realm.

Articles three and four look at Swedenborg's philosophic influences. Francesca Maria

Crasta discusses the metaphysics of Christian Wolff and Gottfried Wilhelm Leibniz on the theme of the soul and its relation to the body. In comparison with Wolff and Leibniz, she argues, Swedenborg's contribution is of interest because it demonstrates the manner by which he attempts to ground his metaphysics within biological principles. Michael Costello continues this exploration by outlining a comparative study of Swedenborg's definition of the soul. He examines Swedenborg's position in relation to wider philosophical discussions on sensation, consciousness, the self and multiple personalities.

Gregory R Johnson, in article five, looks at Schopenhauer's reading of Swedenborg. Returning to the theme of 'spirit-seeing', he argues that Schopenhauer took seriously Swedenborg's writings and the claim that he was a clairvoyant. However, Johnson also goes on to suggest that although Schopenhauer and Swedenborg share the same basic metaphysical outlook, according to which clairvoyance is possible, Schopenhauer's position differs to Swedenborg's insofar as the former claims that the individual soul perishes at death.

The final two articles consider Swedenborg within the light of contemporary philosophic studies. Lars Bergquist, addressing the difficult question of methodology, outlines the contribution Swedenborg's thought might offer to a study of hermeneutics. Swedenborg's method of biblical interpretation, he suggests, renders the text suitable for a comparative phenomenological approach.

Following this article, José Antonio Antón-Pacheco looks at Swedenborg in the light of a distinction between myth and logos. Swedenborg, he suggests, sets out suppositions which are essentially religious, metaphysical, existential and mystical. But he does not just do this with a system (the logos). He puts all these suppositions into a construction that is narrated, has images, and is representive (myth).

The Journal closes with the observation offered by José Antonio Antón-Pacheco that Swedenborg is of interest to contemporary philosophy and poetry because we see in him a storyteller. He is unique insofar as he does not simply retell his experiences of the transcendental in the abstract and conceptual language of categories, but also, importantly, in the concrete form of images and metaphors.

Introduction

Notes

[1] *The Animal Kingdom* [*Regnum Animalis*]. E Swedenborg. pp2-3. First English edition 1843, translated by J J G Wilkinson. The Swedenborg Scientific Association, USA. Reprinted 1960. I have updated the English translation of this passage.

[2] *The New Philosophy* is a journal published by the Swedenborg Scientific Association, centered specifically on Swedenborg's scientific and philosophic writings.

[3] *Swedenborg and Schelling*. F Horn. Translated by G F Dole. The Swedenborg Foundation, USA. 1997.

[4] *The Code of Concord*. A Hallengren. Almqvist and Wiksell International, Sweden. 1994.

[5] *Träume eines Geistersehers, erläutert durch Träume der Metaphysik*, 1766. *The Cambridge Edition of the Works of Immauel Kant: Theoretical Philosophy 1755-1770*. Cambridge University Press, 1992.

[6] *Arcana Caelestia*. E Swedenborg. Translated by J Elliott. The Swedenborg Society Society. 1983-99.

[7] An excellent and primary source for reviewing Swedenborg's debt to other schools of thought can be found in his posthumously published *Philosophers Notebook* 1741-44 (The Swedenborg Scientific Association, 1931), compiled during the publication of his final philosophical work, the *Regnum Animalis*.

Here, one finds Swedenborg quoting extensively from Plato, Aristotle and the early Christian writer St Augustine. The quotations from Augustine are of particular interest, with regard to the later works, because of their explicit Neo-Platonic leanings and their relation to Swedenborg's Science of Correspondences. Only one mention is made of Plotinus himself however, and this is contained in a reference from Augustine, although the former's *Opera Philosophica* was listed in Swedenborg's library from as early as 1705. Extant and frequent references are also made to the work of Nicolas Malebranche. A surprising inclusion concerns three references to Benedict Spinoza's *Principles of Descartes's Philosophy* and the *Ethics*. Elsewhere he quotes Blaise Pascal and Issac Newton, Thomas Aquinas, Cicero, Diogenes and Euclid. He also mentions George Berkeley, Thomas Aquinas, Thomas Hobbes and Montaigne amongst many others. By far the extensive influences on Swedenborg's philosphical works, however, are Gottfried Wilhelm Leibniz, René Descartes and Christian Wolff. For a more comprehensive list of influences one might refer to the index of names listed in his *Principia, Economy of the Animal Kingdom* and *Animal Kingdom*.

[8] *The True Christian Religion*. E Swedenborg. §28. Translated by J Chadwick. The Swedenborg Society, 1988.

[9] *Principia*. E Swedenborg. pp32-33. The Swedenborg Scientific Association. First English Edition 1846. Reprinted 1988.

[10] *Economy of the Animal Kingdom* [*Œconomia Regni Animalis*]. E Swedenborg. p3. The Swedenborg Scientific Association. First English Edition 1843. Reprinted 1960.

[11] ibid.
[12] ibid.
[13] Correspondence with Moses Mendelssohn, April 8, 1766. *The Cambridge Edition of the Works of Immanuel Kant, Correspondence.* Cambridge University Press, 1999.

On the True Philosopher
and the True Philosophy—Essays
on Swedenborg

Swedenborg and Kant on Spiritual Intuition

Michelle Grier

In 1765, Kant published a mysterious work entitled, *Dreams of a Spirit-Seer, as Elucidated Through Dreams of a Metaphysician*.[1] It is well known that the work was motivated by Kant's readings of Swedenborg's *Arcana Caelestia*. Yet, the *Dreams* has long perplexed Kant scholars, who are often stymied by its ironic tone. Because of this, the book has inspired a great deal of speculation, particularly as regards Kant's motives. Was it Kant's intention in the *Dreams* to offer a scathing attack on metaphysics by suggesting that it, like Swedenborg's spiritual experiences, was the product of a delusion? Or was Kant using his 'review' of the *Arcana Caelestia* as a foil in order to ground a deeply Swedenborgian metaphysics all of his own? Many Kant scholars have assumed the first interpretation, although it is certainly clear that some have tried to find in Kant's *Dreams* a veiled endorsement of Swedenborgianism.[2] Interestingly, both of these interpretations find support in Kant's own work, and for good reason. For it seems to me that Kant's position vis-à-vis Swedenborg is neither that of an entirely dismissive critic, nor that of a closet enthusiast. Rather, Kant is conflicted in his response to Swedenborg, and despite his general sympathy for a number of deep-rooted Swedenborgian claims, he remains skeptical on both epistemological and metaphysical, and indeed on moral, grounds of those claims. As Kant himself elsewhere says in speaking of this perplexing work:

> It was in fact difficult for me to devise the right style with which to clothe my thoughts, so as not to expose myself to derision. It seemed to me wisest to forestall other people's mockery by first of all mocking myself; and this procedure was actually quite honest, since my mind is really in a state of conflict on this matter. As regards the spirit reports, I cannot help but be charmed by stories of this kind, and I cannot rid myself of the suspicion that there is some truth to their validity, regardless of the absurdities in these stories and the fancies and unintelligible notions that infect their rational foundations and undermine their value.[3]

I think that it is reasonable to take Kant at his word here, and to accept that he was indeed conflicted in his response to Swedenborg, rather than to try to show either that his support for Swedenborg is entirely dissembled or that he was a closet Swedenborgian who only pretended to have complaints about the latter's methods and testimonies. Even so, the above confession leads one both to inquire into the nature of Kant's agreements and sympathies and to identify precisely the nature of his rejection of Swedenborg's stories. The questions I should like to ask, then, are these: in what way is there 'truth in the validity' of Swedenborg's 'spirit reports'? And exactly what are the 'unintelligible notions and fancies' that undermine their value and 'infect their rational foundations'? Answers to these questions might prove to be illuminating with respect to the relation between Swedenborg and Kant, and may allow us to determine whether Swedenborg's writings provided the basis for any developments in Kant's philosophy. In order to make sense of this issue, we must examine Kant's views about Swedenborg more carefully.

I

As above, the *Dreams of a Spirit-Seer* is a notoriously difficult text to reconcile. Its tone is unusually and, for Kant, uncharacteristically light—almost playfully sarcastic, particularly given the very serious topic with which it is concerned (the doctrine of spiritual being). The tone is just odd enough that straight away Moses Mendelssohn was led to state that 'The jocular profundity with which this little book is written leaves the reader for a time in doubt whether Herr Kant intended to make metaphysics ridiculous or spirit-seeing credible'.[4] In a peculiar preamble, Kant himself seems to exhort his readers not to take the work seriously, indicating again the speculative, undecided and possibly experimental tendencies present in the work, and of which Kant himself was surely aware. Still, Kant seems to be calling into question the legitimacy of metaphysical theories about the nature of spiritual being and its relation to body by juxtaposing them against Swedenborg's own claims as stated in the *Arcana Caelestia*. At issue here is the philosophical conception of spiritual being as *immaterial substance (self-subsistent being)*, a conception that Kant claims leads us into a 'knot'. On the one hand, by virtue of being immaterial, such a being would have to lack the properties of extension, spatial location, and so on. On the other hand, spiritual being is held to be (in some sense) a part of the universe, and to bear some relation to the world of body. In the latter case, it seems spiritual being must be somehow *present*, for how else could a spiritual being bear any relation to body, or exert any influence in the material world? The problems with this last view are commonly, and with no small amount of distress, discussed by academic philosophers and fall under the rubric of the 'Mind Body Problem'. That he was deeply interested in this problem when writing the *Dreams* is confirmed by Kant himself. In a *post facto* explanation of his work to Mendelssohn, Kant states that, 'In my opinion, everything depends on our seeking out data for the problem, *how is the soul present in the world, both in material and in non-material things*'.[5] Indeed, the problem that dominates the *Dreams* is how spiritual being could interact with or bear any relation to body. As such, it has been argued that Kant is concerned with the problems surrounding theories of real influx and potential mind-body interaction that were prominently discussed during the time.[6]

This problem becomes pronounced as Kant moves from the initial and purely philosophical conception of spiritual being above, to chapter two of the *Dreams*. What Kant offers in this chapter is essentially a Platonic or 'two worlds' metaphysical view, i.e. a view according to which 'reality' is divided into two spheres, or worlds: the physical (material) world of our sensuous experience, and the intelligible, or spiritual, world. On the view proposed, a spirit world exists in addition to and alongside of the material world.

But because the material world admits of physico-mathematical (mechanical) explanations only on the basis of the material manifestations of solidity, expansion and form, the spirit world (which has none of these) cannot be explained by appeal to mechanical accounts. Instead, Kant more or less jokingly hypothesises that the spiritual world would have to be governed by a unique set of 'pneumatic laws'.[7] Such laws would have to account for the relation between immaterial beings. More interestingly, Kant suggests that the spiritual world be viewed as the underlying principle of the life that is manifested in the material world. As such, the spiritual world acts as the explanatory ground of the material world. The philosophical outlines of this position, as we later come to see, are characteristic of both the philosophical idealists and Swedenborg, all of whom seek ultimate explanations for phenomena in an intelligible realm. Indeed, it is because of the obvious and explicitly stated similarities between them, that many have come to view Kant's *Dreams* as involving an attempt to discredit metaphysics by suggesting that it is just as 'fanatical' as Swedenborg's spiritual 'fantasies'.[8] Many take this position because it does seem clear that at least part of what Kant is doing is suggesting an analogy between the 'dreams' of the metaphysician, and the 'dreams' of the spirit-seer. And Kant often speaks in ways that seem explicitly hostile to Swedenborg's visions, visions said by Kant to contain 'not a single drop of reason',[9] and to have arisen from a 'fanatical intuition'.[10]

Nevertheless, we must be careful not to misconstrue the reasons why Kant objects to the metaphysical claims of both Swedenborg and the rationalists. Here the above-cited response to Mendelssohn is instructive. Kant repeatedly states in his letter that it is not metaphysics itself, taken 'objectively', that bothers him. Indeed, he emphatically pronounces his high regard for metaphysics. Rather, Kant objects to *the method deployed* by metaphysicians in their efforts to explain things such as spiritual being, or the cause-effect relation. It seems reasonable to suggest that in a similar way, Kant is not necessarily objecting to many of the tenets of Swedenborg's system in their own right. Rather, he is objecting to the ostensible *methods* deployed by Swedenborg to arrive at these. Whereas the metaphysician presumes to arrive at her theses *a priori*, through concepts and principles of an unaided and isolated reason, Swedenborg bases his findings on the interpretation of his own direct spiritual experience. The question for us, then, is why

Kant finds each of these methods (and thus the 'dreams of the metaphysician' and the 'dreams of a spirit-seer') to be inadequate to support the two-world view and the theories of influx they support.

The Problem with the Rationalist Metaphysicians

It might be instructive to consider the problems with traditional, rationalist metaphysics before discussing Kant's complaints about Swedenborg. As above, one problem is clearly that the metaphysician takes the soul to have some kind of 'place' in the world by virtue of which it acts or exerts forces or influences on the body. There are really, it seems, two distinct issues here. The first is a metaphysical problem stemming from the supposed notion of spiritual being as immaterial (a soul with reason), for the metaphysician assigns to an ostensibly immaterial being some kind of real relation to body. To view the soul in this way, however, is to take it to be somehow analogous with body by having some presence or place in the universe. But, as above, the fact that spiritual being is immaterial (simple, non-extended, etc.), poses serious metaphysical problems for the theory. In this regard, Alison Laywine has convincingly argued that Kant's readings of Swedenborg highlighted a number of distinct problems in metaphysics. More specifically, she suggests that Swedenborg's visions illuminated for Kant the dangers stemming from the metaphysicians' tendency to subject immaterial substances to the spatio-temporal conditions under which bodies are given to the senses.[11] The second problem is, it would seem, epistemological, or methodological and relates to the fact that the metaphysician's only way of deducing this consequence is by the use of pure reason, or from concepts alone. Here, Kant's criticism is that the metaphysician presumes to deduce the nature and existence of simple, immaterial beings *a priori*. Such a method is problematic, for Kant, precisely because it involves an attempt to derive conclusions about reality from concepts alone. Already, before the *Dreams*, Kant had developed a criticism of the metaphysicians' presumptions on this score. In both the *Beweisgrund* and the *Deutlichkeit*, Kant had laid the foundations for a criticism of any attempt to use the deductive method in metaphysics.[12] The problem, from Kant's standpoint, is that metaphysics is supposed to be providing knowledge about really existing things (e.g. spiritual beings). Kant's considered view, however, is that formal concepts and principles by themselves cannot deductively yield such knowledge. Indeed, Kant was increasingly of the mind that the deductive method, while appropriate for mathematics, was erroneously deployed by the Cartesians, in their efforts to acquire deductive knowledge of 'reality'.

The force of these criticisms of metaphysical philosophers, as well as the affinity with the presumed errors of Swedenborg, becomes highlighted in chapter three of the *Dreams*. There, Kant mysteriously shifts from the Leibnizian or 'Platonic' perspective of the proponent of any two-worlds view to the more 'Epicurean' perspective according to which reality is co-extensive with what is given in sensation. The latter represents, of course, a more ordinary or 'common sense' standpoint. From this standpoint, however, the notion of spiritual being appears completely unsubstantiated. Given that there are no empirical (intersubjectively accessible) data supporting the theories of spiritual being and spiritual influx, Kant suggests that such theories might be readily dismissed as the solipsistic ego-worlds, or 'dream worlds', of the sleeping. Indeed, in this chapter Kant suggests that, lacking any confirmation by commonly shared sensation or experience, the theories of spiritual being lack credibility altogether. In the *Dreams,* Kant notes that these imaginary philosophical worlds are often constructed through the enthusiastic deductions of the rationalist metaphysicians. It may be that reflecting on Swedenborg's accounts led Kant to the following question: What exactly is the difference between those who think they can access spiritual being by *reason* and those who think they immediately 'perceive' or intuit such being? In either case, the alleged spiritual sphere takes on the characteristic of an 'imaginary world' precisely because it lacks any confirmation by our shared world of experience. Speaking later on of the metaphysicians' deductive method, Kant states without equivocation his concern with the flights of the reason-dreamer: 'This approach involves a new difficulty: one starts I know not whence, and arrives I know not where; the advance of the arguments refuses to correspond with experience'.[13] One problem with the metaphysicians, then, is that in their efforts to 'prove' their theories by appealing to reason alone, they run the risk of having their arguments proceed in *abstracto,* without ever meeting up with experience or factual description.[14] As Kant's critical philosophy began to develop, however, he began to consider the possibility that reason, taken by itself, was 'empty', that it failed to deliver any experiential 'data' that could confirm the substantive metaphysical conclusions it propounded. This concern is articulated throughout the *Dreams*. But Kant goes further. Drawing on earlier developments in his thinking, he suggests that the concept of spiritual being is not only not confirmed by any experiential data, but indeed, that by itself, it provides us with a merely negative conception. To the extent that such a conception has no corresponding data in sensation, we cannot even claim to have any positive definition of what it is we are talking about.

The principle of this life, in other words, the spirit-nature which we do not know but only suppose, can never be positively thought, for in the entire range of our sensations, there are no data for such a positive thought. One has to make due with negations if one is to think something which differs so much from anything of a sensible character. But even the possibility of such negations is based neither on experience, nor on inferences, but on a fiction, in which reason, stripped of all assistance...seeks its refuge.[15]

II

It would be precipitous to conclude from the above concerns that Kant is completely opposed to a Swedenborgian style (two worlds) system. Indeed, many Kant scholars have noted the similarities between Swedenborg's spiritual system and a number of deep Kantian tenets.[16] More specifically, Kant seems to agree with Swedenborg that there is a distinction between the intelligible (or spiritual) and the sensible worlds, and that such a distinction is implicit in the distinction between 'spiritual' and 'material' beings. Here it is important to note that there are deep theoretical reasons that compel Kant's acceptance of the distinction between these two realms. Kant's views on this score coincide with his developing conception of reason as a theoretical faculty. Throughout the *Dreams*, Kant repeatedly indicates that we are rightly compelled by reason to seek ultimate explanations for phenomena in an intelligible (noumenal, spiritual) world. Reason requires that we leap over into such intelligible explanations precisely because the sensible data provided us in experience are insufficient to complete our inquiries. Thus he notes repeatedly, and ironically, that a strictly empiricist view, while perhaps able to explain various experienced (sensuous) phenomena in accordance with mechanical laws, can nevertheless not go beyond such phenomena in order to offer any reason *why* they operate in the ways they do. Although we may, Kant tells us, know from experience that matter operates in accordance with the force of repulsion, we do not know *why* this is so. The answer to our 'why questions' is precisely what reason, in its theoretical use, demands. Kant thus concedes that experience is utterly incapable of yielding sufficient information. Indeed, he recognises that experience itself provides us with grounds for speculating about 'hidden reasons' and underlying principles. As Kant himself notes in another example, the fact that we experience in ourselves abilities that are different in kind from capacities of matter, such as our abilities to think, and to choose, gives us *good reason* to conceive of ourselves as incorporeal and constant beings. The insufficiency of experience, the fact that we are aware that there is 'something left over and unaccounted for', something presupposed by our commonsense 'waking' experiences, is precisely what motivates our reason in seeking ultimate explanations in the intelligible world. Indeed, it is reasonable to assume that this is, at least in part, what Kant meant in his letter to Mendelssohn, when he stated that Swedenborg's 'spirit reports' appear to announce some 'truth', and that they have 'rational foundations'. Or so I contend. For one thing seems certain: despite the views of some commentators, Kant does not argue on behalf of a robust empiricism during this period of his career. Indeed, he does not want to distance himself entirely from the need and demand of reason to seek ultimate (and ultimately intelligible) explanations for the phenomena presented to us in experience.[17]

Since the systems of both the metaphysicians and Swedenborg can be understood to express this deep rational need, Kant is sympathetic. Indeed, Kant agrees that there are reasons which compel us to think the intelligible world 'as a whole' in its own right. As above, he admits that appeals to the intelligible world (and thus spiritual being) stem from the need to 'ground' our material (mechanical) explanations of sensuous phenomena in some intelligible and underlying non-physical source, ground, etc. What we find in the *Dreams*, however, is the view that although reason is legitimate in its demand for ultimate explanations, and although we are in a sense justified in pointing out that there must be something *beyond* experience that ultimately accounts for things, we also must recognise that because sensible experience alone provides the data requisite for (our) theoretical knowledge of reality, reason is incapable of supplying by itself alone such knowledge.

This is indeed the theoretical conclusion drawn from Part I of the *Dreams*. On this score, Kant suggests that the function of reason needs to be reinterpreted. Rather than being the source of *a priori* knowledge about transcendent reality, he suggests, metaphysics is to be viewed as the 'science of the limits of human reason'.[18] Its task is to take the questions highlighted by reason about the hidden nature of things and determine whether such an inquiry even falls within the limits of possible human knowledge.[19] Metaphysics, as a rational inquiry into the nature of things, is thus only in a position to mark out the boundaries of our knowledge. The ultimate suggestion here is that metaphysics (reason) is useful in revealing the boundaries beyond which speculation cannot legitimately go. Specifically, it cannot legitimately pass beyond the domain of experience and, when it does, its claims amount to empty speculation, or fiction.[20] Once again, the need to determine the limits of human reason/knowledge issues from the fact that we are constrained to conceive of and recognise beings that transcend our experience in order to complete our inquiries. The result, however, is a purely negative metaphysics, one that does not presume to offer knowledge of the nature of spiritual being, but which remains content with exposing the limitations imposed by our sensuous experience. The negative doctrine of spiritual being brings our inquiries to completion, not by extending our material knowledge, but rather by demonstrating that we have reached the limits of our perhaps all-too-human knowledge.

The Problem with Swedenborg

Many commentators go to great lengths to emphasise the ways in which Kant might want to liken Swedenborg to the metaphysicians.[21] Nevertheless, if we are to sort through his multi-layered response to Swedenborg, we must be careful to note the way in which Kant *distinguishes* Swedenborg's 'dreams' from the 'reason-dreams' of the metaphysician. Here one thing seems abundantly clear: Kant cannot legitimately criticise Swedenborg for falling victim to the pretensions of reason. In fact, Swedenborg is quite clear in the *Arcana Caelestia* that he takes the systems and arguments of metaphysics to be empty, and inadequate (almost laughably so) for the purposes of illuminating ultimate truths.[22] As we have seen, Kant ultimately seems to agree with Swedenborg on this point, for he argues that metaphysics is only in a position to highlight the boundaries and limits of our human knowledge. Thus, despite Kant's concession that there are 'rational foundations' for Swedenborg's claims (as above), he does not think that Swedenborg errs in exactly the same ways that the metaphysicians do. *If* Swedenborg's claim were simply that he had good reasons to argue for a spiritual world, *if* he claimed to have knowledge of spiritual being simply through the empty deductions of reason, then of course Kant's response to him would be just as it had been to the metaphysicians. But this is, interestingly, *not* Swedenborg's position, and Kant knows it. Swedenborg is not engaging in a purely speculative metaphysics. Rather, his account is essentially a *testimony*, and he claims to access the spiritual world through what we might want to call 'a spiritual faculty', and to have an immediate intuitive experience of such a world.

> In order that I might know that we live after death it has been given me to speak and be in company with many who were known to me on earth; and this not merely for a day or a week, but for months and almost a year, speaking and associating with them, just as in this world. [23]

Kant himself goes to great lengths to distinguish between the case of the reason-dreaming metaphysician and the visionary experiences of Swedenborg. Relevant here is the fact that Swedenborg often seems to testify to having what amounts to something analogous to a sensuous experience of spirits (he 'sees' angels with a spiritual analogue to vision, for example). Indeed, Swedenborg suggests to us that the spirits themselves have sensations; they are said to hear, see, touch, and smell: 'Spirits not only possess the faculty of sight, but they live in such great light that our noonday light can scarcely be compared to it. They enjoy the power of hearing also,...They also possess the power of speaking, and the sense of smell'.[24]

That Kant wants to distinguish between the pretences of the rationalist metaphysicians (the reason dreamers) and the experiences of a Swedenborgian style visionary is abundantly clear in the *Dreams*. For even despite the general similarities noted above (they both presume some access to a transcendent spiritual world, and there are good rational grounds for being motivated in this regard), Kant notes that the dreams of reason are distinctly different from the dreams of the visionary. Kant likens the latter to a kind of 'sensation dreaming'. Unlike the metaphysicians, who arrive at their conclusions from pretensions of reason (precipitous judgments), the spirit-seer actually experiences spirits in what amounts to something analogous to sensation. Because of this, the spirit-seer is unable to banish his visions simply by reasoning them away, for 'true or illusory, the impression of the senses itself precedes all judgment of the understanding and possesses an immediate certainty'.[25]

These considerations illuminate, perhaps, the way in which ruminating on Swedenborg's visions provided the basis for the development of some important Kantian doctrines. It may also highlight the precise nature of Kant's disagreement with Swedenborg. The main puzzle presented by Swedenborg has to do with the latter's claim to have immediate or direct (intuitive) experience of the spiritual world. This is especially puzzling insofar as Swedenborg's 'visionary' experiences include visual, auditory, tactile (i.e. sensible) experiences. Kant's *Lectures on Metaphysics* suggest little concern with the most general possibility that we may be capable of having both a sensible and a 'spiritual' intuition. Indeed, as we shall see Kant refers to Swedenborg's claim that we are members in both an intelligible and sensible world as 'sublime'. Nevertheless, Kant does seem to find certain problems with Swedenborg's claim to have both of these *at once*. Even more specifically, it seems to me that most of Kant's derision is reserved for the suggestion that Swedenborg is having essentially sensible representations of immaterial beings.[26] For how could an immaterial being be intuited sensibly? Kant's view seems to be something like this: either you've got a spiritual intuition, or you've got a sensible one. You cannot have the two simultaneously. In conjunction with this, Kant's first complaint relates to Swedenborg's claim to access this spiritual world while *still in the body*. Consider the following:

But one question still remains: whether the soul, which already sees itself spiritually in the other world, will and can appear in the visible world through visible effects? This is not possible, for matter can be intuited only sensibly and fall only in the outer senses, but not a spirit. Or could I not to some extent already intuit here the community of departed souls with my soul, which is not yet departed, but which stands in their community as a spirit? e.g. as Swedenborg contends? This is contradictory, for then spiritual intuition would have to begin already in this world.[27]

Despite Kant's endorsement of many 'Swedenborgian' themes, his central disagreement with Swedenborg has to do, it seems, with our 'mode of access' to the 'spiritual world'. On this, Kant's charge is that Swedenborg claims to access the spirit world directly while still in the sensible world. In this, from a Kantian standpoint, Swedenborg has assumed to possess some kind of spiritual or mystical intuition that Kant claims we simply do not have, at least so long as we are beings governed by a sensible intuition. This view stems from Kant's epistemology, developing at the time of the *Dreams*, and fully developed in the later *Inaugural Dissertation* (1770). Kant's position is that objects are given to the human mind in accordance with a faculty of receptivity, or 'intuition'. According to Kant, our only mode of intuition is 'sensible', and it is governed by the pure 'forms of sensibility', space and time. Clearly, a spiritual being, which is immaterial, is not spatial in the sense that allows it to be intuited.

It is in connection with this problem that Kant tentatively develops a theory of metaphysical delusion in the *Dreams*. Kant suggests that the subjection of immaterial being to sensible conditions that characterises both the metaphysician and Swedenborg might spring from and share in a deception indicative of the illusory experiences characteristic of dream states. This last suggestion clearly reflects Kant's growing concern to trace the conclusions of metaphysics back to their source in the human mind. One similarity between the metaphysician, the visionary and the 'dreamer' stems from the fact that in all cases, an individual believes herself to access an 'objective' world, a world of really existing and mind-independent things, despite the fact that such beings are not inter-subjectively accessible from the common, ordinary (sense-based) experiences of everyone else. The experiences of the visionary, in particular, share with dreaming states the quality of seeming to 'see' and 'hear' (etc,) objective phenomena, despite the fact that there are no inter-subjectively accessible objects that would allow us to confirm the experience. Kant indicates that from a common sense standpoint, one could argue that the pretence to have access to the spiritual realm might be just as deluded as experiences grounded in 'diseases of the brain'.[28]

I should like to suggest that Swedenborg's accounts provided Kant with a striking example of the capacity and tendency of the human mind to transpose ideas and subjective experiences into objects that have mind-independent status. Later in his career Kant comes to argue that metaphysics stems from certain illusions of the mind.[29] This claim links up to the afore-mentioned notion that reason demands ultimate explanations, the data for which can never be met with in any sensuous experience. The result is that we are compelled to postulate intelligible grounds (e.g. spiritual beings) to account for what is given in our experiences. Kant becomes increasingly preoccupied with the way in which the human mind is led to 'hypostatise' these ideas, to ineluctably take them to be objective beings (objects) that provide the basis for our explanations. Indeed, it is interesting to note that the full-blown theory of metaphysical illusion so dominant in Kant's critical work (i.e. the *Critique of Pure Reason*) is tentatively laid out in the *Dreams* for the first time. There, Kant is deeply concerned to ask how it is that we come to take subjective phenomena (ideas of reason, subjectively experienced visions, etc.) and take them to be things that have real (mind-independent) existence:

> Hence, the question I wish to have answered is this: How does the soul transpose such an image, which it ought, after all, to present as contained within itself, into a quite different relation, locating it, namely, in a place external to itself among objects which present themselves to the sensation which the soul has.[30]

Note that this phenomenon of 'transposing' subjective experiences 'as objects'[31] is not dismissed by Kant as ridiculous. Nor is such a tendency simply characteristic of 'fanatics' and charlatans. What seems to interest Kant is the utterly commonplace feature of this, for each of us does this all the time whenever we dream. The similarity of visionary and dream states, in which we find ourselves 'talking' and as it were 'sensing' objects and others who are not, presumably, actually present in any mind-independent fashion, provided Kant with the materials for these reflections. It seems to me, indeed, that Swedenborg's testimonies offered Kant with the material for a deep rumination on the overwhelming tendencies of metaphysicians to engage in their own abstract form of spirit-seeing. These considerations might allow us to refine our views about the nature of Kant's ambiguous response to Swedenborg.

It seems at times that Kant's point is that any theory of real relation that applies to both material and immaterial beings is doomed because it involves what Kant later commonly refers to as a 'subreption'. A subreption, for Kant, indicates a fallacy according to which we surreptitiously substitute concepts and terms of one kind for those of another. For Kant, the term is usually reserved for cases where we conflate concepts and principles of sensuous experience with those of pure reason. In the case at hand, Kant is concerned with a subreption according to which the immaterial beings or souls are construed by analogy with material, physical beings.[32] At issue here is the metaphysician's strained efforts to account for real interaction by surreptiously viewing spiritual being as analogous to physical being, in order to make sense of the alleged capacity to exert spiritual influences on body. More importantly, we find the general suggestion that metaphysicians (and particularly the metaphysical theories about the soul) erroneously presume to have access to spiritual being in a way that is analogous to the way we can access material objects. The metaphysician, in short, must presume to have some sort of direct *intellectual* (*rational*) access to the spiritual world in the same way that Swedenborg claims to access such a realm through a *mystical* intuition. This is precisely Kant's complaint. Indeed, the claim in the *Dreams* that there are no data corresponding to reason's pure concepts foreshadows the famous Kantian doctrine that our (human) reason is not intuitive. To state the later formulated and well-worn Kantian dictum: 'Concepts without intuitions are empty; intuitions without concepts are blind'. Or, in other words, according to Kant, we (unlike, say, God) do not have intellectual intuition. Since intuition is the capacity to be affected by and 'given' objects, Kant's real suggestion (albeit nascent in the *Dreams*) is that human intuition is in all cases sensible. The result is that, from a Kantian standpoint, the theories about spiritual being lack the epistemological support required to ground them. It is thus not surprising to find that in the main work published after the *Dreams*, Kant develops his doctrine of metaphysical error. By the later *Inaugural Dissertation* (1770), Kant had come to a full characterisation of the illusions of the intellect, and a theory of 'subreption'.

III

The story does not stop here, however. Note that the thrust of the critical remarks offered by Kant relate to our *theoretical* efforts to acquire knowledge of the transcendent world. That is, Kant is clearly interested in drawing a boundary beyond which speculation and knowledge cannot go. It was in this connection, it seems, that he suggested that the 'dreams' (whether they be those of the metaphysician or the visionary) cannot serve as justified theoretical accounts. But Kant leaves opaque his actual position here. In chapter two, he suggests that the proliferation of ghost stories could equally well be explained by the fact that we *are*, each of us, truly in relation to the spiritual world.[33] In this, Kant seems to recognise that his own theoretical conclusions pertaining to metaphysics, i.e. the claims about limiting reason in its speculative or theoretical aims, leave open a number of issues relating to the moral theory. It may indeed be that Swedenborg's writings also highlight the distinction between reason in its theoretical and its moral (practical) uses, for even despite the above, Kant does not seem to want to reject a number of Swedenborgian claims. That we are each of us always already participants in the intelligible world, that each 'person' is, by virtue of a moral subjectivity (a soul) always already in communion with all other moral subjects, and that it is correct to view ourselves as subjects who participate in such a community, these are things which Kant surely seems to find attractive. Similarly, Kant does not dismiss the suggestion that heaven and hell are not 'places' to which we somehow find ourselves transported after death, but are rather the spiritual conditions reflected in the nature of our soul, or reflecting the degree of our moral development. It may, then, be that ruminating on Swedenborg's views, which place a primacy in moral, spiritual intuition (rather than simply on 'knowledge' from reason alone) led Kant to recognise that practical (moral) reason makes its claims upon us despite our theoretical limitations. And indeed, that it must do so. Here, it is interesting to note that throughout the *Dreams* Kant indicates that all the speculative tendencies of the metaphysician might actually find their real source in, and ultimately be guided by, practical (moral) interests. Moreover, the practical conclusion of the *Dreams* suggests that the speculative fairy-spinnings of the metaphysician are ultimately 'superfluous and unnecessary' for moral purposes. This in turn suggests that Kant might find some 'truth in the validity' of Swedenborg's accounts without countenancing use of Swedenborg's visions as evidence for any metaphysical knowledge.

Kant's agreement with many of the Swedenborgian theses is confirmed in the *Lectures on Metaphysics*, and it is here that Kant's emphasis on moral considerations in praising Swedenborg become most pronounced. Throughout these *Lecture*s one finds Kant simultaneously praising and criticising Swedenborg. Kant's agreements stem from his concession that there is a real (i.e. metaphysical) distinction between the bodily or sensuous world on the one hand and the spiritual world on the other. Kant also agrees with Swedenborg that our bodily existence is governed by sensible intuition, which clouds and conceals our participation in the spiritual world. Consider the following:

> We have a cognition of the bodily world through sensible intuition insofar as it appears to us...but when the soul separates itself from the body, then it will not have the same sensible intuition of this world; it will not intuit the world as it appears, but rather as it is. Accordingly the separation of the soul from the body consists in the alteration of sensible intuition into spiritual intuition; and that is the other world.
>
> ...the thought of Swedenborg is in this quite sublime. He says the spiritual world constitutes a special real universe; this is the intelligible world [*mundis intelligibilis*], which must be distinguished from this sensible world [*mundo sensibili*]. He says all spiritual natures stand in connection with one another, only the community and connection of the spirits is not bound to the condition of the bodies...Now as spirits our souls stand in this connection and community with one another, and indeed already here in this world, only we do not see ourselves in this community because we still have a sensible intuition; but although we do not see ourselves in it, we still stand within it. Now when the hindrance of sensible intuition is once removed, then we see ourselves in this spiritual community, and this is the other world; now these are not other things, but rather the same ones, but which we intuit differently.[34]

As we have seen, Kant cannot and does not want to go so far as to concede that Swedenborg's testimonies provide the basis for any theoretical knowledge of the spiritual realm, life after death, and so on. Thus, he refrains from accepting Swedenborg's testimonies for the reasons cited above, i.e. the subreptive conflation of conditions of sensation and reason. However, Kant often seems to find in Swedenborg thoughts that are 'sublime' as expressions of a moral subjectivity. Given this, we might wonder why Kant would want to shy away from Swedenborg's testimonies. Does Kant have good reason to deny the reliance on mystical or immediate experience of a spiritual world, especially as expressions of an attuned moral (spiritual) subjectivity? And if so, what exactly are his reasons? Kant is quite explicit about admitting that Swedenborg's experiences, like the dreams of the metaphysician, can neither be confirmed nor disproved. Once again, however, Kant seems to think in the *Dreams* that in the face of our inability to confirm or deny, we must grant the rights to experience:

> If, however, certain alleged experiences cannot be brought under any law of sensation, which is unanimously accepted by the majority of people, and if, therefore, these alleged experiences establish no more than an irregularity in the testimony of the senses (as is, in fact, the case with the ghost stories which circulate), it is advisable to break off the enquiry without further ado, and that for the following reason. The lack of agreement and uniformity in this case deprives our historical knowledge of all power to prove anything, and renders it incapable of serving as a foundation to any law of experience, concerning which the understanding could judge.[35]

In the face of these considerations, it appears that Kant's only recourse is to suggest that Swedenborg's alleged experiences do not constitute sufficient *evidence* or grounds for the spiritual system he promotes. While Kant is not (admittedly) in a position to disprove Swedenborg's claims, he nevertheless feels that a reliance on such subjective and unique experiences might undermine reliance on more secure methods, not only in the theoretical philosophy, but in issues of morality. Indeed, Kant's deeper fear seems to be that a full-scale embrace of Swedenborg's accounts opens the floodgates to a mystical fanaticism or enthusiasm which Kant finds particularly worrisome. It is worrisome in some sense because it might possibly undermine the ethical position it seeks to express. One danger is that it might engender the conflation of ground and consequence. More specifically, Kant's claim is that we should not act morally in order to increase our chances of a blissful afterlife, but should, rather, cultivate a moral disposition which in turn leads to a noble hope for the future.[36] Thus, our need to 'prove' the existence of an afterlife, a spiritual realm, either by metaphysics or by reliance on Swedenborg's assurances, displaces the real ground of morality: 'What, is it only good to be virtuous because there is another world? Or is it not rather the case that actions will one day be rewarded because they are good and virtuous in themselves? Does not the heart of man contain within itself immediate moral prescriptions? Is it really necessary, in order to induce man to act in accordance with his destiny here on earth, to set machinery moving in another world?'.[37] What Kant fears is the encroaching 'enthusiasm' of mysticism or the fanaticism that he is concerned it may engender. Kant thus concludes:

Nor has human reason been endowed with the wings which would enable it to fly so high as to cleave the clouds which veil from our eyes the mysteries of the other world. And to those who are eager for knowledge of such things and who attempt to inform themselves with such importunity about mysteries of this kind, one can give this simple advice: that it would probably be best if they had the good grace to wait with patience until they arrived there.[38]

Notes

[1] *Träume eines Geistersehers, erläutert durch Träume der Metaphysik*. Immanuel Kant. 1766. Passages from the *Dreams* are taken from *The Cambridge Edition of the Works of Immanuel Kant: Theoretical Philosophy 1755-1770*. pp. 301-359. Cambridge University Press, 1992.

[2] I do not mean to suggest that these two broadly opposed positions exhaust the ways in which scholars have attempted to account for Kant's response to Swedenborg. In fact, even within these two camps, sholars differ on exactly how they interpret Kant's position. For a good summary of some of these, see Alison Laywine, *Kant's Early Metaphysics and the Origins of the Critical Philosophy, North American Kant Society Studies in Philosophy, Volume 3*. Ridgeview Publishing Company: Atascadero, California, 1993.

[3] Correspondence to Moses Mendelssohn, April 8, 1766, in *The Cambridge Edition of the Works of Immanuel Kant, Correspondence*. Cambridge University Press, 1999.

[4] *Gesammelte Schriften,* second series, vol. 4. Moses Mendlessohn. p529. Edited by G B Mendelssohn, Leipzig. F A Brockhaus, 1844.

[5] *Correspondence*, p. 91.

[6] Alison Laywine, see especially pp. 55-100.

[7] Kant suggests in his letter to Mendelssohn (1766) that his analogy between a real moral

influx by spiritual beings and the force of universal gravitation is 'not intended seriously; it is only an example of how far one can go in philosophical fabrications.' See *The Cambridge Edition of the Works of Immanuel Kant: Correspondence,* p. 92.

[8] See for example, Kuno Fisher, *Geschichte der neuern Philosophie*, volume four. Heidelberg. Carl Winters *Universitätsbuchhandlung*, 1898. For a detailed discussion of this kind of reading, see Laywine, pp. 19-21.

[9] *Dreams*, p. 346.

[10] *Dreams*, p. 347. For a more detailed discussion, see my *Kant's Doctrine of Transcendental Illusion*. Cambridge University Press, 2001.

[11] Alison Laywine, *Kant's Early Metaphysics*, especially chapters 4 & 5. Laywine's position is essentially that Kant's readings of Swedenborg highlighted the way in which his (Kant's) early metaphysics, and particularly his theory of real influx, committed him to the possibility of a Swedenborgian account. Kant, seeing this similarity between his own and Swedenborg's views is said by Laywine to have been deeply disturbed. I agree with much of what Laywine contends, but feel that Kant's response was considerably more complex and ambiguous than she suggests.

[12] See *Der einzig mögliche Beweisgrund zu einer Demonstration des Daseins Gottes* of 1763 and *Untersuchung über die Deutlichkeit der Grundsätze der natürlichen Theologie und der Moral* of 1764.

[13] *Dreams*, p. 344.

[14] *Dreams*, p. 345.

[15] *Dreams*, p. 339.

[16] As an example, see Hans Vaihinger, *Kommentar zu Kants Kritik der reinen Vernunft*, second edition, volume two. Stuttgart. Union Deutsche Verlagsgesellschaft, 1992.

[17] And, interestingly, one might note that the following work, *The Inaugural Dissertation*, develops even more fully this notion of the intellect as a theoretical faculty, and argues for the possibility of a non-fallacious metaphysics through the use of the concepts of the intellect. See *The Cambridge Edition of the Works of Immanuel Kant: Theoretical Philosophy, 1755-1770*, pp. 373-415.

[18] *Dreams*, p. 354.

[19] *ibid*.

[20] For a fuller treatment of this issue, see my *Kant's Doctrine of Transcendental Illusion*. Cambridge University Press, 2001. p. 43.

[21] Depending on the commentator, one finds the broad suggestion that either 'Swedenborg is to be taken just as seriously as the respectable metaphysicians,' or 'the metaphysicians are just as fanatical as Swedenborg.'

[22] *Arcana Caelestia*. E Swedenborg. §3348. Trans. John Faulkner Potts, Fourth American Edition, New York. Swedenborg Foundation, 1949.

[23] *Arcana Caelestia* §70 as presented in *Swedenborg: Life and Teaching*, by George Trobridge,

The Swedenborg Foundation, New York, 1992.

[24] *Arcana Caelestia* §322 as presented in *Emanuel Swedenborg, Essential Readings*, by Michael Stanley, Biddles Limited, 1988.

[25] *Dreams*, p. 335.

[26] In this respect, we may agree with Laywine, that Kant is concerned with the problems associated with subjecting immaterial being to the spatio-temporal conditions under which objects of the senses are given.

[27] The passage is taken from *The Cambridge Edition of the Works of Immauel Kant: Lectures on Metaphysics*, p. 106. Cambridge University Press, 1997.

[28] See my *Kant's Doctrine of Transcendental Illusion*. pp. 32-40.

[29] I argue at length for the claim that Kant's theory of metaphysical error is linked up with this propensity to hypostatise and project subjective ideas as objects. See my *Kant's Doctrine of Transcendental Illusion*.

[30] *Dreams*, p. 331.

[31] *Dreams*, p. 331.

[32] This use of the term is also found in Kant's Lectures. See Blomberg Logic in *The Cambridge Edition of the Works of Immanuel Kant: Lectures on Logic.* p. 203. Cambridge University Press, 1992.

[33] *Dreams*, p. 322.

[34] *Lectures on Metaphysics* p.104.

[35] *Dreams*, 2:372; p358.

[36] *Dreams* p. 359.

[37] *Dreams* p. 358.

[38] *Dreams* p. 359.

Swedenborg's *Positive* Influence on the Development of Kant's Mature Moral Philosophy*

Gregory R Johnson

Kant's rigorous and sublime system of ethics, with its emphasis on universality, consistency, autonomy, and duty for duty's sake, is one of the greatest contributions ever made to moral philosophy. 'Kantianism' is so firmly ensconced in the textbooks as one of the timeless moral archetypes that, aside from a few specialist scholars, there is very little understanding of the development of Kant's moral thinking and the figures who influenced it.[1] Wolff, Crusius, Shaftesbury, Hutcheson, Hume, and especially Rousseau are the chief influences cited. Leibniz and Pope are cited as the primary influences on Kant's thoughts about theodicy, a topic closely connected to his moral philosophy. But Swedenborg is seldom taken seriously as an influence on Kant's moral philosophy, even though it is in *Dreams of a Spirit-Seer*, Kant's 1766 book on Swedenborg, that the outlines of Kant's mature moral philosophy first emerge.[2] I wish to argue that Swedenborg did in fact influence the development of Kant's moral philosophy. This influence was, furthermore, a positive one, meaning that Kant arrived at his mature position not merely by rejecting, but by incorporating, elements of Swedenborg's thought.

1. Kant's Copernican Ethics

The first stage in the development of Kant's moral philosophy is what I shall dub his 'Copernican Ethics,' which I detect in his writings from 1754 to 1759, primarily his *Universal Natural History and Theory of the Heavens* (1755)[3] and his second essay on the great Lisbon earthquake of 1755, 'History and Natural Description of the Most Remarkable Occurrences Associated with the Earthquake...' (1756).[4] Kant's ethics in this period is 'Copernican' not in the sense of Kant's Copernican Revolution, but of *Copernicus's* Copernican Revolution. First, it presupposes the modern, post-Copernican vision of the cosmos in which God seems remote, his providence attenuated, and nature inhospitable to the human good. Second, just as Copernicus solved the astronomical problem of the organisation of the solar system by imagining how it would look from a cosmic, rather than an Earth-centered point of view. Kant seeks to solve moral problems by recommending that we look at the human condition from a cosmic, rather than an anthropocentric point of view.

Kant's Copernican ethics is an attempt to reconcile human beings to a distant God and an inhospitable universe. It is, therefore, a theodicy: an attempt to defend the justice of divine providence by answering the classical problem of evil: How do we reconcile divine omniscience, omnipotence, and omnibenevolence with the existence of evil? This perennial philosophical problem is much intensified by the modern image of an inhospitable, mechanistic cosmos in which the achievement of value is constantly threatened by the contingencies of matter and, in the long run, is extinguished under the rule of the iron law of entropy, which dictates that all order and motion will be extinguished.

In chapter seven of his *Universal Natural History*, Kant attempts to reconcile us with this grim picture by offering us a series of cosmological hypotheses. The common thrust of all these hypotheses is to induce a sense of complacency and reconciliation by inducing the reader progressively to displace himself from the perspective of a human being suffering under the reign of contingency. One can wrest some meaning from one's suffering only by finding a higher vantage point, from which one's own misfortunes can be subsumed into the larger patterns of nature. Kant's cosmological hypotheses lead us to higher and higher vantage points, wider and wider perspectives on the cosmos, greater and greater distances from the human condition, until at last cosmological reason gives way to faith and we gain a sense of what it would be to grasp the whole from the perspective of God Himself. A similar argument is offered in the closing pages of the second earthquake essay. According to Kant's Copernican ethics, we shall cease to feel the pains of the human condition by detaching ourselves from it and identifying ourselves with the larger economy of nature and the inscrutable will of God.

Kant's Copernican ethics is not only characterised by the centrality of the theodicy problem and the moral priority of the cosmic point of view over the human point of view. It is also characterised by a concern with the hierarchical arrangement of different cognitive types. This shows up in two ways. First is Kant's 'elitist' dependence upon theoretical reasoning achievable only by the few, as opposed to practical reasoning achievable by all. Second, part three of the *Universal Natural History* is devoted to the unusual topic of extraterrestrial intelligent beings, specifically those inhabiting the other planets in our solar system (an interest shared by Swedenborg).[5] This section is significant for two reasons. First, Kant arranges the different dwellers of the planets in a hierarchy based on the relative strengths of their cognitive powers. (Human beings come out in the middle, but some of us are closer to our betters and some of us closer to our inferiors than others). Second, although Kant is concerned with hierarchy and difference, he does have an expansive, cosmic conception of a community of rational beings that includes more than just humans.

2. Rousseau and the 'Ptolemaic' Counter-Revolution

I shall dub the second stage of the development of Kant's moral philosophy the Ptolemaic counter-revolution[6] in morals, which I detect in the writings of 1760 to 1765, particularly the *Observations on the Feeling of the Beautiful and Sublime* (1764),[7] the 'Essay on the Sicknesses of the Head' (1764),[8] and the so-called *Remarks* of 1764-65, that Kant penned in his own copy of the *Observations*.[9] I call it 'Ptolemaic' because just as Kant's Copernican ethics proposes to solve the problems of human existence by encouraging us to displace ourselves from the point of view of the human actor to that of a cosmic spectator, the Ptolemaic counter-revolution reasserts the primacy of the human point of view over the cosmic. This is accompanied by the corollary assertion of the primacy of the practical reason of the human agent over the theoretical reason of the cosmic spectator. Because practical reason can be exercised by virtually all human beings, whereas high levels of theoretical attainment are open only to the few, this stage also marks a move from an unabashed intellectual elitism to a more egalitarian and populist moral outlook.

The grounds for this egalitarian move are already present, albeit latently, in Kant's cosmology. In the *Universal Natural History*, Kant observes that, 'All that is finite, whatever has limits and a definite relation to unity, is equally far removed from the infinite'.[10] Kant's reasoning is that, in the face of an infinite universe, all finite differences—including finite human differences—are ultimately matters of indifference; or, as Kant puts it, 'in the presence of the infinite, the great and small are small alike.'[11] This reasoning is beautifully encapsulated in the story of 'Carazan's Dream', that Kant quotes in a footnote in the *Observations*:

One evening, as I drew up my accounts and calculated my profits, sleep overpowered me. In this state I saw the Angel of Death come over me like a whirlwind...I was led before the throne of the third heaven. The glory that flamed before me spoke to me thus: "Carazan, your service of God is rejected. You have closed your heart to the love of man, and have clutched your treasures with an iron grip. You have lived only for yourself, and therefore you shall also live the future in eternity alone and removed from all communion with the whole of Creation". At this instant I was swept away by an unseen power, and driven through the shining edifice of Creation. I soon left countless worlds behind me. As I neared the outermost end of nature, I saw the shadows of the boundless void sink down into the abyss before me. A fearful kingdom of eternal silence, loneliness, and darkness! Unutterable horror overtook me at this sight. I gradually lost sight of the last star, and finally the last glimmering ray of light was extinguished in outer darkness! The moral terrors of despair increased with every moment, just as every moment increased my distance from the last inhabited world. I reflected with unbearable anguish that if ten thousand times a thousand years more should have carried me along beyond the bounds of all the universe I would still always be looking ahead into the infinite abyss of darkness, without help or hope of any return. In this bewilderment I thrust out my hands with such force toward the objects of reality that I awoke. And now I have been taught to esteem mankind; for in that terrifying solitude I would have preferred even the least of those whom in the pride of my fortune I had turned from my door to all the treasures of Golconda.[12]

Carazan, by limiting his perspective merely to the human realm, brought human differences, both natural and social, into the foreground. Consequently he was an elitist, a miser, a misanthrope. However, once he was exiled from the human world and cast into the sublime and infinite void, all such differences lost their importance. In the presence of the infinite, great and small became small alike.

The Ptolemaic stage of Kant's ethics could also be called Rousseauian, for although its basic principles were latent in Kant's earlier works, it was Rousseau who provided the decisive stimulus to Kant's thinking.[13] Kant records this influence in a famous *Remark* from 1764 or 1765:

I am by inclination an inquirer. I feel in its entirety a thirst for knowledge and a restless desire to increase it, along with satisfaction in each forward step. There was a time when I thought that this alone could constitute the honour of mankind, and I despised the people, who know nothing. Rousseau set me right. This blind prejudice vanished. I learned to honour human beings, and I would be more useless than the common worker if I did not believe that this view could give worth to all others to establish the rights of mankind.[14]

Rousseau taught Kant that, contrary to the best hopes of the Enlightenment—indeed, contrary to the intellectualism of virtually the entire philosophical tradition—intellectual excellence does not automatically equal moral excellence; intellectual progress does not necessarily equal moral progress; in fact, the progress of the arts and the sciences leads, in most cases, to the increase of human unhappiness by corrupting those virtues that are more likely to be found in simple, uneducated souls.[15] The theorist's claim of moral superiority vanishes. It is important to note, however, that neither Kant nor Rousseau ever deny the ineluctable fact of intellectual inequality. They deny only that intellectual inequality is equivalent to moral inequality. Because theoretical activity is no longer regarded as necessarily or intrinsically good, it must justify itself by serving a moral purpose. The sole justification of theoretical activity becomes the service it renders to the moral and practical interests of mankind.

Kant's Rousseauian turn is characterised by a broadening of his ethical interests beyond the theodicy problem to such issues as the grounds of moral obligation and the springs of moral motivation. Another important result of Kant's encounter with Rousseau—one that is especially important in setting the stage for his encounter with Swedenborg—is his formulation of the idea of 'laws of freedom' (*Gesetzen der Freyheit*). From a strictly Newtonian materialist point of view, the laws of nature govern a wholly deterministic system of physical monads, and freedom is a violation of physical law; the idea of 'laws of freedom' is, therefore, an oxymoron. Rousseau, however, identifies human goodness with both nature and freedom, implying simultaneously that human nature is not deterministic and that human freedom is law-governed. A true-bred materialist would simply have rejected such notions outright. Kant, however, did not. Instead, Kant declared Rousseau to be the Newton of the moral world:

> Newton was the first to see order and regularity bound with great simplicity; whereas before him disorder and badly joined multiplicity was encountered, since then the comets run in geometrical courses.
>
> Rousseau was the first to discover under the multiplicity of available human forms [*Gestalten*] mankind's deeply hidden nature and the concealed law through which providence through its observation is justified. Before, the objection of Alphonso and Mani was valid. After Newton and Rousseau, God is justified and henceforth Pope's teaching is true.[16]

Kant's declaration that Rousseau is the Newton of the human world does, however, create a problem: How does the human world, with its laws of freedom, fit into the physical world, with its laws of necessity?

Kant's *Remarks* also record a serious engagement with Rousseau's identification of nature and goodness, i.e., his attempt to ground moral obligation in human nature. Kant also adopted Rousseau's understanding of human nature as free, unified, and self-determining. As Kant puts it: 'The question is whether, in order to move the affects of myself or others I should take my point of support from outside the world or within it. I answer that I find it in the state of nature, that is, in freedom'.[17] In order to reconcile the freedom, unity, and autonomy of the state of nature with the constraint, alienation, and heteronomy of the civil condition, Kant also adopted Rousseau's distinction between human beings as products of nature and human beings as products of history:

> ...by *man* here I do not only mean man as he is distorted by the mutable form [*Gestalt*] which is impressed upon him by the contingencies of his condition, and who, as such, has nearly always been misunderstood even by philosophers. I rather mean the unchanging *nature* of man, and his distinctive position within the creation...This method of moral enquiry is an admirable discovery of our times, which, when viewed in the full extent of its program, was entirely unknown to the ancients.[18]

Rousseau claimed that the move from the state of nature to the civil condition was merely a matter of contingency, not the result of natural teleology or providence. Neither the push of our nature nor the pull of our destiny requires that man become civilised. Our hearts are just not in it. This asocial conception of man's nature gives Rousseau the vast critical distance and leverage needed to undertake a total critique of civilisation. Kant, however, claims that human beings are driven into society by a natural sociability.[19] But he still retains a sufficient critical distance from the modern civil condition to offer a radical, Rousseauian critique.[20]

Like Rousseau, however, the aim of Kant's critical project is not to return us to the state of nature. This is impossible. History cannot be undone. We must try to uncover our natural state in order to put ourselves in a position outside of society. From this position, we can take stock of both the losses suffered and the gains made in our passage from nature to civilisation: 'If one evaluates the happiness of the savage, it is not in order to return to the forests, but in order to determine what one has lost while in other respects one has made gains'.[21] From this position, we can also take up the task, not of destroying, but of reforming the restraints of civilisation, bringing them in harmony with our natural sentiments. The purpose of *Emile*, claims Kant, is to show the way 'to remain a man of nature in society.'[22] This is Kant's purpose as well: 'My purpose will be to establish which perfection is appropriate to him [man] in the state of *primitive* innocence and which perfection is appropriate to him in the state of *wise* innocence'.[23]

To combine natural freedom and civilised constraints, Rousseau recommends that we discover those constraints that we can freely impose upon ourselves. The set of all such laws constitutes an ideal republic. Insofar as the human will naturally and necessarily wills the good, it naturally and necessarily wills this republic. Rousseau calls this will the General Will. It is what all of us, deep down, truly will. Individual human beings can bring our empirical wills into harmony with the General Will (our true wills), only by paring away the countervailing forces of irrational desires and passions. Kant too adopted this account of the moral will, and he never abandoned it. In the *Groundwork of the Metaphysics of Morals*, Rousseau's General Will appears as Kant's Holy Will: the will that necessarily wills the good. Individual human beings can bring our wills in line with the holy will by surmounting our sensuous and selfish impulses and subordinating them to the good.

Another important feature of Kant's writings of this time is his serious exploration of the relationship of morality and feeling, a task prompted by Rousseau's claim that knowledge of the natural goodness of man is accessible through the sentiments of self-esteem and pity, and Kant's populist concern to connect moral knowledge to levels of cognitive attainment available to all human beings. It is at this point in his career that Kant began his engagement with the British moral sense theorists, particularly Shaftesbury, Hutcheson and Hume.

Kant's doctrine of 'moral feeling' (*moralische Gefühl*) is, however, problematic. Feelings are clearly rooted in our physical natures. Our physical natures, however, are clearly subject to the amoral laws of nature, not the moral laws of freedom. 'Moral feeling', seems, therefore, to be as oxymoronic as 'laws of freedom'. Furthermore, feeling, insofar as it can be said to be moral at all, is traditionally associated with eudaimonistic ethics. Kant, however, does not think that the pursuit of happiness is the true aim of morality. Indeed, duty often requires that we be willing to sacrifice our happiness for the sake of goodness. It is this ability to sacrifice happiness for goodness, to contravene the incentives of the entire economy of nature to heed the higher call of duty, that constitutes for Kant the true ground of human moral self-esteem. Finally, the relationship of moral feeling to the General Will is quite problematic, for it seems that we align our individual wills with the General Will only insofar as we rise above our feelings. The General Will is the same as our autonomy. Feelings, moral or otherwise, are a principle of heteronomy. How the latter are compatible with the former is unclear.

A final feature of Kant's Rousseauian turn to the human perspective is his constriction of the morally relevant community: from the *Universal Natural History*'s community of *rational beings as such* to the specifically *human* community. Virtue becomes identified with 'universal affection toward the *human* species' and 'a high feeling of the dignity of *human* nature'.[24]

3. Swedenborg and the Turn Toward the Supersensible

Kant's early writings display an unresolved tension between two principles that he regarded as equally true. On the one hand, he was completely convinced that the world, including the human body, is a complex machine, a completely determinate system of material bodies that can be understood solely in terms of mathematical physics and requires no recourse to such explanatory principles as teleology, special providence, or spiritual influxes, including the free will. On the other hand, Kant was equally convinced of the freedom, dignity, and moral responsibility of human beings, a conviction that he received at his mother's knee and that was powerfully reinforced in his thirties by his encounter with the writings of Rousseau.

But how does the human world, with its laws of freedom, fit into the physical world, with its laws of necessity? Moral freedom and complete physical determinism cannot exist in the same world. The laws of nature and the laws of freedom cannot be reconciled within a single system. Something has to give. Susan Shell nicely sums up the problem of Kant's Rousseauian ethics:

> The 'Remarks'…leave us with two principles of world 'unity', two forces of 'attraction' whose relation remains unresolved: a 'natural instinct of active benevolence' rooted in sexual desire (and inequality), and a non-instinctual benevolence associated with

the free community of equals...The first is 'indeterminate' and destabilising, but also dynamic; the second is determinately bound up with the timeless concept of a perfected moral/political whole.[25]

My suggestion is that Kant resolved these problems through a creative appropriation of Swedenborg.

In *Dreams of a Spirit-Seer*, part I, chapter two, Kant offers an account of the spirit world that he claims is based solely on his own speculations—although, he adds, it just happens to be confirmed by Swedenborg's visions. It is clear, however, that the two correspond so closely because Kant's account of the spirit world is nothing more than a careful philosophical reconstruction of Swedenborg's.[26] Kant argues for the existence of the spirit world based on the following phenomena: (1) the existence of non-material, non-locatable animating principles (souls), (2) the existence of a *sensus communis*, which leads us to submit our judgments for intersubjective adjudication, and (3) the existence of distinctly moral motivations, which lead us to thrust aside our private, selfish, and sensuous motivations and take up a universal standpoint. Kant argues that these phenomena can best be explained by positing the existence of a spirit world. Kant claims that the spirit world is inhabited by essentially the same kinds of beings as Swedenborg does:

> This immaterial world would...include, firstly, all created intelligences, some of them being united with matter so as to form a person, others not; the immaterial world would, in addition, include the sensible subjects in all animal species; finally, it would include all the other principles of life wherever they may exist in nature...All these immaterial natures, whether they exercise an influence on the corporeal world or not, and all rational beings, of which the animal nature is an accidental state of their being, whether they exist here on earth or on other heavenly bodies, and whether they are now animating the raw stuff of matter, or will do so in the future, or have done so in the past—all these beings, I say, would, according to this account, stand in a community consonant with their nature.[27]

Kant, like Swedenborg, claims that the spirit world consists of a systematic unity or whole of spiritual beings: 'these immaterial beings, if they are directly united, may perhaps together constitute a great whole, which could be called the immaterial world (*mundus intelligibilis*)'.[28] Since spirits account for the phenomena of life and moral obligation, which cannot be reconciled with causal determinism, Kant, like Swedenborg, concludes that they must have causal laws of their own: 'The particular causal laws in terms of which they operate are called *pneumatic*, and, in so far as corporeal beings are the mediating causes of their effects in the material world, they are called *organic*'.[29] Like Swedenborg, Kant also claims the spirit world would exist outside of space and time: 'This community would not be based on the conditions which limit the relationship of bodies. It would be a community in which distance in space and separation in time, which constitute the great chasm in the visible world which cancels all community, would vanish. The human soul, already in this present life, would therefore have to be regarded as being simultaneously linked to two worlds'.[30] Finally, Kant claims that some people in this life can gain the knowledge available to their spiritual selves, a knowledge unlimited by the conditions of space and time, by means of decoding the meanings of influxes from the spirit world that clothe themselves in spatio-temporal garb. Kant's account is essentially identical to Swedenborg's.

This Swedenborgian vision of the spirit world suggested to Kant his solution to the problems of Rousseau's ethics. From the premise that moral freedom and physical determinism cannot exist in the same world, Kant concluded that if he was to preserve both freedom and determinism, he would have to split the world in two, and this he did, dividing the whole into material and spiritual, sensible and intelligible, or phenomenal and noumenal worlds. The phenomenal 'world' is the world insofar as it is given to the senses, a realm of beings perceived as in space and time and interpreted by the categories of the understanding. It is a wholly deterministic system of material bodies governed in accordance with physical laws. The noumenal 'world' is that aspect of the world that is not given to any form of intuition, sensible or intellectual, but that is only intelligible or thinkable. Whereas phenomena are always sensuously given in space and time, noumenal or intelligible beings are given independent of space and time. The noumenal realm comprises a number of things. First, all beings have a noumenal aspect just insofar as their existence transcends our consciousness of them, i.e., just insofar as their being is not exhausted by their being present to us. Second, the noumenal realm, like the phenomenal realm, is a system, a community of spiritual monads governed by pneumatic laws.

Human beings are citizens of both worlds. Insofar as we are phenomenal beings, we are members of the community of physical monads wholly determined by Newtonian laws. If, however, human beings were *merely* natural beings, we would not possess freedom, dignity, and moral responsibility. But the experience of freedom, dignity, and moral responsibility is undeniable. We find ourselves stirred by a feeling of respect for the moral law, the commandments of which might contravene the entire economy of nature; we can thrust aside the incentives of pleasure and pain, glory and shame, even the desire for self-preservation itself to heed the call of the moral law. Insofar as we can do this, we experience a dimension of ourselves that transcends the entire natural order. This noumenal dimension is our moral personality; it is the locus of freedom, dignity, and moral responsibility; it establishes our citizenship in the kingdom of rational beings governed by spiritual laws. In his mature works, Kant refers to this spiritual realm as the 'moral world', the *'corpus mysticum'* (the mystical body), the *'regnum gratiae'* (the Kingdom of Grace), the *'mundus intelligibilis'* (the intelligible world), and the 'Kingdom of Ends' (*Reich der Zwecke*).[31] It is the realm that Swedenborg claims to have seen and heard.

Kant's Swedenborgian ethics continues his Ptolemaic counter-revolution. The chief difference is that Kant retracts his 'humanist' identification of the moral community with mankind alone and reasserts his earlier, expansive account of the moral community as including all rational beings as such, expanding it even further to include not just extraterrestrials, but the spiritual aspects of embodied beings, disembodied spirits, and—taking Swedenborg as our guide—perhaps angels and demons as well.

The continuities, though, are striking. First of all, Kant's Swedenborgian ethics preserves his Rousseauian emphasis on the priority of practical reason over theoretical reason, and of the moral agent's point of view over that of the scientific spectator and technological operator. Kant, however, strips the agent's point of view down to its moral essence. He does not return to a full-blown classical teleological interpretation of nature. Kant does hold that the teleological interpretation of nature and history is absolutely essential, but he also holds that it is underdetermined by empirically accessible phenomena and can be grounded only in a form of reflective judgment that ventures out beyond what can be sensuously verified. Kant thus leaves in place the mechanistic interpretation and technological mastery of nature. (The primacy of the spirit world is not the primacy of the life-world.) In short, Kant's discovery of the spirit world reverses the moral meaning of the first Copernican Revolution, while leaving its scientific meaning intact. Kant reasserts that man's true home, the spiritual world, is still the center of the universe (morally speaking), even though our material home is but a mote whirling in the void.

Second, Kant's Swedenborgian ethics preserves his Rousseauian concern with the questions of moral justification and moral motivation. However, in opposition to Rousseau and the moral sense theorists, Kant abandons any attempt to account for moral justification and motivation by reference to feelings, for all feelings belong to our *material* nature, which is wholly determined by physical laws and thus falls outside of our moral personality. Kant does, however, preserve Rousseau's General Will and the reciprocal laws of love and respect that it legislates. But he transforms them into pneumatic laws of the spiritual world. Furthermore, Kant preserves a notion of moral feeling in the form of the feeling of respect (*Achtung*) for the moral law and for rational natures, but Kant claims that the feeling of respect is *not* a feeling in the physiological, and therefore materially determined, sense. Finally, it must be noted that Kant's Swedenborgian ethics lays the groundwork not only for Kant's mature moral philosophy, but for the *Critique of Pure Reason* as well. Kant's own Copernican Revolution—which itself is Ptolemaic insofar as it asserts the epistemological primacy of the human point of view—is made necessary by his Ptolemaic revolution in morals. In order to establish the primacy of the moral agent's point of view, i.e., the primacy of practical reason, Kant must rein in the imperialistic ambition of theoretical reason to be the sole source and criterion of truth; Kant must limit (theoretical) reason to make room for (moral) faith. Hence it is no accident that Kant first refers to the project of a critique of pure reason in *Dreams*, as well as in texts and reflections composed at the same time, in 1764-65.[32]

Conclusion: The Starry Heavens and the Moral Law

To conclude this account of Swedenborg's role in the development of Kant's mature moral philosophy, I wish to examine Kant's own conclusion to the *Critique of Practical Reason*, where—his victories secured—he looks back upon his struggles.

> Two things fill the mind with ever new and increasing admiration and awe, the oftener and more steadily we reflect upon them: the starry heavens above me and the moral law within me...The former begins at the place I occupy in the external world of sense, and it broadens the connection in which I stand into an unbounded magnitude of worlds beyond worlds and systems of systems and into the limitless times of their periodic motion, their beginning and their continuance...The...view of a countless multitude of worlds annihilates, as it were, my importance as an animal creature, which must give back to the planet (a mere speck in the universe) the matter from which it came, the matter which is for a little time provided with vital force, we know not how.[33]

This is the question. The cosmos revealed by modern science annihilates our freedom, dignity, and self-esteem. How, then, do we retain our humanity?

The answer is our citizenship in another world, a community of spiritual beings, free, rational and dignified, existing under laws of spiritual harmony and perfection; this spiritual community transcends the material world in both fact and value; it therefore serves as the archetype for the progressive transformation of nature and society in its image. In Kant's words:

> The latter [the moral law] begins at my invisible self, my personality, and exhibits me in a world [i.e., the spiritual world] which has true infinity but which is comprehensible only to the understanding [i.e., it is intelligible or noumenal]—a world in which I recognise myself existing in a universal and necessary (and not only, as in the first case, contingent) connection, and thereby also in connection with all those visible worlds [insofar as these other visible worlds are homes to rational beings]...The latter [citizenship in the spiritual world]...infinitely raises my worth as that of an intelligence by my personality, in which the moral law reveals a life independent of all animality and even of the whole world of sense—at least so far as

it may be inferred from the purposive destination assigned to my existence by this law, a destination which is not restricted to the conditions and limits of this life, but reaches into the infinite.[34]

The answer, in short, is Swedenborg.

Notes

[*] This is a heavily-revised version of a lecture delivered to the Swedenborg Seminar of the American Academy of Religion at their annual convention in Philadelphia, on November 18, 1995. I wish to thank Professor Jane K Williams-Hogan of the Academy of the New Church College in Bryn Athyn, Pennsylvania for inviting me.

[1] On the development of Kant's moral philosophy, see Paul Menzer, 'Entwicklungsgang der kantischen Ethik in den Jahren 1760-1785,' *Kant-Studien* 3 (1899):41-104; Josef Schmucker, *Die Ursprünge der Ethik Kants in seinen vorkritischen Schriften und Reflexionen* (Meisenheim: Anton Hain, 1961); Dieter Henrich, 'Hutcheson und Kant,' *Kant-Studien* 49 (1957): 49-69; 'Über Kants früheste Ethik,' *Kant-Studien* 54 (1963): 404-31; *Aesthetic Judgment and the Moral Image of the World: Studies in Kant* (Stanford: Stanford University Press, 1992); Paul Arthur Schilpp, *Kant's Pre-Critical Ethics* (Evanston: Northwestern University Press, 1960); Keith Ward, *The Development of Kant's View of Ethics* (New York: Humanities Press, 1972); Richard L Velkley, *Freedom and the End of Reason: On the Moral Foundation of Kant's Critical Philosophy* (Chicago: University of Chicago Press, 1989); Susan Meld Shell, *The Embodiment of Reason: Kant on Spirit, Generation, and Community* (Chicago: University of Chicago Press, 1996); and J B Schneewind, *The Invention of Autonomy: A History of Modern Moral Philosophy* (Cambridge: Cambridge University Press, 1998).

[2] Two significant exceptions are Keith Ward in *The Development of Kant's View of Ethics* and 'Kant's Teleological Ethics,' in *Immanuel Kant: Critical Assessments*, ed. Ruth F. Chadwick, 4 vols. (New York: Routledge: 1992), III, 244-46, and J N Findlay in *Kant and the Transcendental Object: A Hermeneutic Study* (Oxford: Clarendon, 1981), 76-7. According to Findlay, '[Swedenborg's] spiritual world [is] perhaps the original of Kant's 'kingdom of ends',' (76) and 'We are obviously here [in *Dreams*] anticipating the kingdom of ends of which so much is made in the *Metaphysic of Morals* [sic], and it is pleasing to know that this conception, though rational, is also mystical and Swedenborgian' (77). The majority view, however, is represented by Schneewind, who sums up *Dreams of a Spirit-Seer* by saying, 'Well, it was not

meant seriously' *(The Invention of Autonomy*, 505). The greatest obstacle to taking seriously the possibility that Swedenborg influenced Kant is the snide and flippant tone of *Dreams*. I offer an explanation of the literary qualities of *Dreams* and argue at length that Kant was decisively influenced by Swedenborg in my doctoral dissertation, A Commentary on Kant's *Dreams of a Spirit-Seer*, (Washington, DC: The Catholic University of America, 2001).

[3] Kant, *Universal Natural History and Theory of the Heavens*, trans. W Hastie (Ann Arbor: University of Michigan Press, 1969) (a partial translation that leaves out the book's entire third part) and *Universal Natural History and Theory of the Heavens*, trans. Stanley L Jaki (Edinburgh: Scottish Academic Press, 1981) (complete).

[4] Kant, 'History and Physiography of the Most Remarkable Cases of the Earthquake which Towards the End of 1755 Shook a Great Part of the Earth', in Kant, *Essays and Treatises*, 2 vols., trans. John Richardson (London: William Richardson, 1798-99), vol. 2:95-142.

[5] See Emanuel Swedenborg, *The Earths in Our Solar System which are Called Planets and the Earths in the Starry Heaven and their Inhabitants; also the Spirits and Angels There; from Things Heard and Seen*, trans. J Whitehead (New York: The Swedenborg Foundation, 1913). This book contains excerpts from the articles appended to the chapters of the *Arcana Coelestia* which deal with the book of *Exodus*. We know that Kant read this material, for he refers to it in one of his lecture courses: *Fragment einer späteren Rationaltheologie nach Baumbach*, AK 28.2,2:1325.

[6] I wish to thank John Gerard Moore for this phrase.

[7] Kant, *Observations on the Feeling of the Beautiful and the Sublime*, in Kant, *Essays and Treatises*, vol. 2:1-78 and *Observations on the Feeling of the Beautiful and Sublime*, trans. John T Goldthwait (Berkeley: University of California Press, 1960).

[8] Kant, 'Versuch über die Krankheiten des Kopfes,' AK 2:257-71.

[9] Kant, *Bemerkungen zu den Beobachtungen über das Gefühl des Schönen und Erhabenen*, AK 20:1-192; henceforth cited as *Remarks*.

[10] *Universal Natural History*, Hastie, 139.

[11] *Universal Natural History*, Hastie, 136.

[12] *Observations*, Goldthwait, 48-9, n.

[13] There are a number of excellent studies on the influence of Rousseau on Kant, particularly as reflected in the *Remarks* of 1764-65. See Schmucker, *Die Ursprünge der Ethik Kants in seinen vorkritischen Schriften und Reflexionen*; Ernst Cassirer, 'Kant and Rousseau' in his *Rousseau, Kant, Goethe*, trans. James Gutmann, Paul Oskar Kristeller, and John Herman Randall, Jr. (Princeton: Princeton University Press, 1945); Dieter Henrich, 'Über Kants Entwicklungsgeschichte' *Philosophische Rundschau* 13 (1965): 252-63; Richard L Velkley, *Freedom and the End of Reason*; and Susan Shell, 'Kant's Political Cosmology: Freedom and Desire in the 'Remarks' Concerning *Observations on the Feeling of the Beautiful and the Sublime*,' in *Essays on Kant's Political Philosophy*, ed. Howard Lloyd Williams (Chicago:

University of Chicago Press, 1992); see also chapter 4 of her *The Embodiment of Reason*.

[14] *Remarks*, AK 20:44.

[15] See especially Jean-Jacques Rousseau, *Discourse on the Sciences and Arts* (First Discourse) (1751), trans. Judith R Bush and Roger D Masters, in *The Collected Writings of Rousseau*, vol. 2, ed. Roger D Masters and Christopher Kelly (Hanover and London: Dartmouth College/ University Press of New England, 1992).

[16] *Remarks*, AK 20:58-9. On the project of Newtonian moral philosophy, cf. the conclusion to Kant's *Critique of Practical Reason*, trans. Lewis White Beck (Indianapolis: Bobbs-Merrill, 1956), 167-8.

[17] *Remarks*, AK 20:56.

[18] Kant, *M. Immanuel Kant's Announcement of the Programme of his Lectures for the Winter Semester of 1765-1766*, trans. David Walford, in Immanuel Kant, *Theoretical Philosophy, 1755-1770*, ed. and trans. David Walford with Ralf Meerbote (Cambridge: Cambridge University Press, 1992), AK 2:311-12; Walford, 298; henceforth cited as *Announcement*.

[19] On this contrast, see Shell, 'Kant's Political Cosmology', 89.

[20] See, for example, the opening pages of the 'Versuch über die Krankheiten des Kopfes', AK 2:257-8.

[21] *Remarks*, AK 20:31.

[22] *Remarks*, AK 20:31.

[23] *Announcement*, AK 2:312; Walford, 298.

[24] *Observations*, Goldthwait, 58, 66, emph. added.

[25] Shell, 'Kant's Political Cosmology', 105.

[26] Kant circumspectly admits to this point in *Dreams*, AK 2:257-9; Walford, 344-5. On this point, see also Robert H Kirven, 'Swedenborg and Kant Revisited: The Long Shadow of Kant's Attack and a New Response,' in *Swedenborg and his Influence*, ed. Erland J Brock, et. al. (Bryn Athyn, Pennsylvania: The Academy of the New Church, 1988), esp. 114. See also C D Broad, 'Kant and Psychical Research,' in his *Religion, Philosophy and Psychical Research*, 2nd ed. (New York: Humanities Press, 1969), 143.

[27] *Dreams of a Spirit-Seer Elucidated by Dreams of Metaphysics*, trans. David Walford, in *Theoretical Philosophy*, AK 2:332; Walford, 319; henceforth cited as *Dreams*..

[28] *Dreams*, AK 2:329; Walford, 316-17; Kant's parentheses.

[29] *Dreams*, AK 2:329; Walford, 316-17.

[30] *Dreams*, AK 2:332; Walford, 319.

[31] Kant refers to the moral world/*corpus mysticum*/*regnum gratiae* in the *Critique of Pure Reason*, A808/B836. He refers to the Kingdom of Ends/*mundus intelligibilis* in the *Foundations of the Metaphysics of Morals*, trans. Lewis White Beck (New York: Macmillan, 1990), 49-57 (AK 4:433-8).

[32] *Dreams*, AK 2:369; Walford, 355; *Remarks*, AK 20:181; *Announcement*, AK 2:310-11.
[33] *Critique of Practical Reason*, AK 5:162; Beck, 166.
[34] *Critique of Practical Reason*, AK 5:162; Beck, 166.

Metaphysics and Biology: Thoughts on the Interaction of the Soul and Body in Emanuel Swedenborg

Francesca Maria Crasta

This paper will approach Swedenborg from a historical/philosophical perspective. It is possible that this might strip some of the mystery or allure from Swedenborg's own works which depend to a large degree on a conception of spiritual reality. This is a risk that emerges whenever one tries to discuss works which, over time, have been shown to contain literary as well as philosophic considerations. The historian of philosophy however, is committed to the study of the content/language of the texts and their place in a precise philosophical and cultural context.[1]

The priority of any historical/philosophical study is to understand an author's place alongside his contemporaries. In the case of Swedenborg, this involves the way in which he is linked to the climate and mood of the Enlightenment, even if his voice or influence extends further. In the absence of such a perspective, we may find him difficult to understand, or worse, unable to piece together the parts of the tapestry which at first glance might appear disjointed. The dissonance between a text and context can often lead to forced interpretations, loading a work with meanings that are not always legitimised by the text and which evaporate into the literary. This could be detrimental to a clearer understanding of a text, of locating and referencing it accurately within an historical and philosophical context.

With this in mind, this paper will restrict itself to a modest study of a transitional phase of Swedenborg's philosophy between his youthful and mature experiences. Yet to be studied are the passages from the *Oeconomia Regni Animalis* [*Economy of the Animal Kingdom*] which arguably contain his most organic and complete discussion of the biological problems involved in the interaction of the body-soul discussion.[2] This can be referred to in the second part of the second volume in which Swedenborg considers in depth the nature of the soul. Here he throws light on a series of issues which were at the centre of the seventeenth and eighteenth century debate, involving the more general problem of the organic deriving from the inorganic. My intention will be to indicate materials which might be useful to the completion of a definition of its historical framework. I will leave it to others to outline an exhaustive reconsideration of the eighteenth century discussions on this theme, especially as seen in the wake of the considerable impact of this problem on contemporary philosophical debate.[3]

Swedenborg's references to the soul-body relationship can be found in a series of treatises beginning in 1719 and ending in 1769 with the completion of *De Commercio Animae et Corporis* [*The Interaction of the Soul and Body*].[4] The continued return to this theme shows the importance of the problem to his wide and varied philosophical work, which—as is known—ranges from mineralogical research and cosmology to the exegesis of sacred texts. One clear reference to this issue is found in the first part of the first volume of his *Opera Philosophica et Mineralia* [*Principia*], published in 1734,[5] a work dedicated to the analysis of the means by which man can attain real knowledge. Swedenborg observes that man is *ad sapientiam continuo aspirat* [continually aspiring towards wisdom] and identifies three courses for realising this end: *secundum experientiam* [according to experience], *secundum geometriam* [according to geometry] and *secundum facultatem ratiocinandi* [according to the faculty of reason]. The *sine qua non* for reaching this end is that the soul is conveniently connected to the sense organs which enable a relationship or flow of information between inner and outer worlds. A series of reflections follow this observation, and two facts clearly emerge. In the first instance he cites a strict connection (*nexus*) between body and soul. In fact, the movements from the outer world are perceived by the sense organs and are transmitted by contact and connection to the soul. He describes the movement of stimulations from membranes or denser media (*media crassiora*) to finer ones (*subtiliora*), which brings about a continuous flow of small vibrations or 'tremulations'. In the second instance—and emerging from this discussion concerning the destination and convergence of the movements transmitted by the sense organs to the soul—the soul is then described as material, although it is in this case a very fine and active material.

These considerations seem to indicate an affinity with the Cartesian philosophical tradition. The problem of sensation is approached as a mechanical phenomenon, that is, as a simple process of transmission of movements through media of varying thicknesses and densities. Moreover in his 1719 *Anatomi af wår aldrafinaste natur* [*On Tremulation*],[6] Swedenborg indicates a series of 'fixed' and 'indubitable' laws that regulate movements in organic bodies, which he believes to be basically analogous to those of the most minute parts of inorganic matter. With reference to his theory on the movements of living things, he writes:

> ...every part of what is living in the body lives by means of little tremulatory motions which flow into the nerves and the membranes and set the whole system into sympathetic tremulation; and as soon as a contremiscence is distributed over a whole body, it may be termed a sense or a sensation, and that if all the contremiscences of the senses are taken conjointly, they possess the same name of nature, *or of life.*[7]

This theory is also clarified in his letters to Eric Benzelius during this period. In February 1724 he attempts to explain how movements of vibrations originate and propagate in the organism:

> I assert that *tremulation* begins in *liquido* [liquid] or in *fluido membranaceo* [fluid membrane], so that, if there is to be any spreading, the *membranae* [membrane] must be tensed both with their *duro* [hard element, i.e. bone] and with the *vasis sanguineis* [blood vessels] for thus all the *vasa lymphatica* [lymphatic vessel] or *vasa fluidi nervei* [fluid nerve vessels] in *membraneis* [the membranes] lie in their proper condition and, like all else, the fluid in accordance with its *contiguum, premerar* [contiguous pressure] almost *in istanti* [instantly], and thus brings the *membranas*

[membranes] into *tremulation* with itself, and these their *ossa*, [bones] so that almost the whole body comes into a subtle quivering which give sensation.[8]

What is interesting in all this is that Swedenborg tries to find a logical line that connects the inorganic and organic worlds in a single structure, thus recognising analogous characteristics to be investigated with the same criteria and methods. It is no coincidence that in the 1719 text quoted above, he constantly repeats that living and inanimate bodies obey identical laws. Every body is in fact subject to 'tremulations' which on the smallest impact diffuse through the surrounding environment. These movements can be perceived by the sense organs which transmit them through a complex series of membranes working as transmission organs for the vibrations, inside the organism up to the brain where they are translated into mental data.

But in the 1734 text, cited before, it is interesting to note Swedenborg's reference to the *anima*, which he defines as 'something active and very subtle'[9] indicating that it is material. In fact the manuscript titled *De Mechanismo Animae et Corporis* (*Mechanism of the Soul and Body*) and probably of the same period,[10] points to the same conclusion. In this work, Swedenborg affirms the naturalness of the soul whilst also underlining the importance of the contiguity and reciprocity of the movements[11] connecting the internal and external. The soul, as such, like any other natural entity, can then be studied via the laws of mechanics and geometry.[12] He justifies this assertion by stating that it is impossible to indicate otherwise than that the soul is created, that it belongs to the world of finite entities and that it is therefore generated from those natural points. It is nevertheless the first entity directly derived from the infinite, and as such, a pivot of Swedenborgian metaphysics:

It will have either space or figure, or the likeness or appearance of space and figure, therefore no other rules are possible than mechanical and geometrical ones; if not, it would be something of the infinite, it would be something of the non-create; if it be bound by rules, they cannot be other ones than those which arise from geometry; therefore it is natural.[13]

In the next paragraph Swedenborg goes on to state that the soul is in reality formed by the active entities of the first and second finite entities, and that these active entities circumscribe little spaces around which the passive ones are arranged. In his opinion, this is the only way to explain the origin of the soul. It is formed by the first natural elements—that is, the first determinations deriving from the metaphysical point—so it can only be the most minimal natural element and also the most active and elastic. These observations enable him to attribute to the soul a sort of figure and space, however minimal, which let the soul immediately perceive movements and alterations which the other membranes and nervous tissues in the organism register in relation to the external impressions and the passions of the body.[14]

Thus, the interaction between the body and soul, consists of the contiguity of the parts and reciprocity of movements described by Swedenborg as movements of compression and expansion is ensured.[15] If the soul is diffused throughout the body, one must also note that it is above all present in all the fibrous and membranous parts in the brain.[16] In fact we find the most complex structure of nerves and membranes inside the brain cavity. This is the privileged site of the soul:

...the soul is especially spread through the whole brain, so that there is no part in the whole brain where the soul is not, as well in the cortical as in the medullary [portion], as also in the bony portion, as whatever is in the brain ends in the soul, on which account the soul invests all the mechanical parts, and thus it acts by compression and dilatation into the organic and mechanical parts of the body.[17]

It is interesting to note that the soul is not destroyed when the organism dies. The soul simply changes state and transforms into a sort of conglomeration (*conglomeratus*). It is subtle and elastic and so cannot be dissolved in the air or destroyed by fire,[18] and because of this peculiar physical constitution it is destined never to perish.

All this could imply that Swedenborg was inclined to believe in a materialistic model whereby any natural phenomenon including the soul would have to be investigated using only mechanical dynamics and processes. However, this interpretation is complicated by Swedenborg's own statement that should prevent any dangerous slide towards the atheism that a solid materialism would arrive at. Rather, it is precisely an understanding of the relationship between body and soul that may lead us to recognise the existence of an infinite being and the very immortality of the soul:

> *...if we postulate the soul as a something most unknowable and secret and something far removed from sense; this is the nearest road to atheism and naturalism.* We see that there is mechanism in such things as can be examined ocularly, and therefore we may conclude that there is also mechanism in things more subtle; but we do not understand what mechanism this may be, and because we do not understand, and the world does not wish that the matter should be understood, therefore we remain in the most obscure darkness concerning it, and we believe that it is something of the infinite, whence we confuse the infinite, and suppose that the soul herself is a similar unknown something like the infinite, and that consequently the infinite is like the natural, or natural like the soul...It may be added that the more deeply we proceed into the knowledge of nature, the greater light do we come into, as it were from the darkness itself into a knowledge of the deity, which we can thus in no way deny; thus natural philosophy will lead us truly to confession of the infinite.[19]

The question then arises as to how is it possible to admit that the soul is immortal and material at the same time? How can something be defined as material and immortal together?

To resolve this difficulty, Swedenborg resorts to one of the dominant themes of his philosophy of nature: the relationship between infinite and finite, God and the world. This is a theme rich in implications which he develops while trying to extend some of the categories already used in the *Principia* to the field of psychology. A clear understanding of the soul-body relationship for Swedenborg means recognising on the one hand that everything which is finite and created is knowable, whilst on the other acknowledging the existence of an absolutely unknowable creator which cannot be accessed by the instruments of reason. Reason is certainly powerful (as an instrument of progress and investigation), but it is finite and limited, and as such is also derived from that original point which indicates the beginning of the world and the origin of everything that man can know.

In his *Prodromus Philosophiae Ratiocinantis de Infinito, et Causa Finali Creationis: deque Mechanismo Operationis Animae et Corporis* [*The Infinite and Final Cause of Creation*],[20] dedicated to Benzelius and published at roughly the same time as the *Principia* (1734), he picks up on the theme of the interaction between body and soul again, and while he reaffirms the concept of infinity as being exclusively divine, he also confirms that the soul is finite, created and therefore causally derived from God.[21] Once it is established that the soul is a finite entity that operates in connection with another finite entity, the body, it is necessary likewise to set the rules and laws by which such connection is concretely effected. Again, the rules and laws are those of mechanics and geometry.[22] These are said to govern all phenomena, from heavenly phenomena to that which is hardly perceptible to the sense organs which the microscope reveals more and more accurately. Nature is a homogenous whole in which the same laws and principles are at work[23] throughout.

The soul, therefore, presents itself not as a substance ontologically separate and distinct from the body, but rather, as one integral to it and able to perform more than one function in the whole organism in which it is situated. It interacts with the body in an immediate way. Swedenborg defines the soul as a *quid activissimum* [something active], and states[24] that its nature is not different from the other active entities described in the fifth and seventh chapters of the first part of the *Principia*. For this, its activity must be circumscribed with its own kind of membrane, which can only exist in its relationship with the periphery formed by the finite passive entities. This way the soul is recognised as having its own duplex nature because it is made up of active and finite entities. For this reason it is able to act, move and determine, but also to notice, perceive and feel. If it was pure activity, it would not be able to receive and feel the stimuli that come from outside, and so would not be able to react to them. He states:

...assuming that the soul is a simple, a pure, and a most perfect active; finite, however, in its simplicity, purity, and perfection; it remains to be seen how this predication would coincide with its essence and attributes. If the activity of the soul consists in these, it must necessarily be such that it can act upon the parts of its own body exclusively; that it can suffer and receive the motions or modes arising from the body;

that it can dispose or adapt itself thereto; and afterwards reflect them, and meet the forces acting upon it by a corresponding reaction, so as to be adapted at least to produce such modes, and this, within the sphere and space of the bodily system. If the soul were merely an active of this kind, it might indeed act, but it could not be in itself sentient of the actions of the body, nor dispose itself for reception at the same time as for action, nor modify itself to the different parts of the body. The complement of its essence requires then something beyond pure activity; in short, a passive principle, adequate to enclose or shut its actives in a definite space, or, if we may use the expression, in a passive expanse; whereby it may not only be enabled to act on the body, but also to receive the actions arising from the body; also to adapt itself to the variety of modes, and reflect them back again; a passive principle, we repeat, in which the soul may be able to exert its actuality and power; and which, in a word, will ensure passivity to the soul as well as activity. [25]

These indications underline the idea that the soul belongs to the world of nature and as such is an integral part of an organism that for Swedenborg, primarily, is a machine. And since it is part of a composite and mechanical whole, it will also be *mechanica et geometrica*.[26] At this point Swedenborg is keen to introduce a definition of this analogy between soul and machine. But this is not to be done *cum machinis inanimatis sed cum animatis* [as mechanically inanimate but as animate].[27] In fact the soul has many and particularly complex faculties: *ut imaginandi, percipiendi, concludendi, memoria tenendi, coscientia sui, prout vocatur, ideae reflexae et plura alia possent explicari* [for instance: imagination; perception; the power of conclusion; memory; self consciousness and the ideas of reflection etc., etc.,].[28] Animals possess these as well, but in an imperfect and less distinct form. Its material is so subtle and elastic—with a mechanism so perfect—that it is immortal,[29] and therefore does not suffer the vicissitudes of the body after death.

Swedenborg clarifies that the very nature of the soul and its aims, consist in recognising the existence of the infinite and the desire to reach a state of greater perfection which only an immortal soul, free from the destiny of the body, can conceive. This is different from many philosophers who relegate the activity of the soul to that of the animal spirits.[30]

To demonstrate this immortality of the soul, he offers a series of considerations:

> We may also deduce and conclude analytically and rationally from the nexus of natural beings and things in the world, that the soul or subtlest part of the body must be immortal. For as the soul is in the purer and more perfect realm of nature, and the body in the less perfect, it follows that the soul cannot be obnoxious to change like the grosser bodily parts; and that it resembles the more immutable nature, as it has the power both to act and suffer, and to conform in every manner to the entities of that sphere, so as like them to enjoy the most complete immunity from change. But the immortality of the soul is declared by facts presented in our very bodies. For love, with its delicious sense, which is purer as the nature is purer, arises simply from the harmonious connection of natural parts. It is afterwards derived *per nexum* into the grosser parts of the body, that is to say, into the less perfect sphere of the animal world, where it has again the same end, namely, of conferring perpetual life in a certain sense on the body also.[31]

The soul still participates in the transformations of the body, but keeps its own natural perfection intact. It is not contaminated or corrupted by the world in which it is located and to which it is connected through the specific mode of contiguity. Such connection—as a relationship of contiguity between entities—also implies the sharing of space, which according to the strictest mechanical meaning of the term *connexio* (connection), implies the concept of a contact, a tangency, *materialiter* (materiality) meant between single bodies and parts. No movement can be noticed and no event can occur in the world of finite entities[32] without contiguity, which ensures the existence of connections between all the parts, according to a continuous and successive scale of degrees. These degrees are already defined in the *Principia*, where Swedenborg sets out a 'mapping' of the inorganic world which is articulated according to a series of passages that connect the physical with the metaphysical, the finite with the infinite through the mediation of the impulse points. This scheme is put forward again, largely unchanged, in a different and particularly complicated context, to construct a network of connections and correspondences going from the biological to the psychic, the physiological to the mental.

The transmission of wave motion, through the series of this kind of membranes enables the soul to receive, in a physical way, the messages coming from the outside.[33] The final destination or point of convergence of all vibrations is the brain: the seat of the rational soul and centre of the peripheral terminations. Here the membranes become so fine that the movements that flow together in it become noticeable and therefore clearly distinguishable according to their harmony or disharmony. The structure of the brain is in fact characterised as an extremely complicated and ramified series of tissues and membranes that enclose the cortical substance and even penetrate futher within. It can therefore, he suggests, *praecipue*, be chosen as the specific seat of the rational:

> Not so, however, in the cerebrum, all whose parts are enveloped with their peculiar tunics, and the tunics and membranes that are visible, and the still larger number that are invisible, can and do ramify in an eminent manner; from which it is fair to conclude, that the seat of the rational soul is in an especial sense in the brain, and does not extend beyond it. In the cerebrum we have the pia mater, a very fine and visible membrane covered with innumerable blood vessels, and which ramifies again and again, and detaches tendons of the finest make, as well as an exquisitely delicate contiguity of membrane; all which dip into and pervade the cerebrum, and ultimately pass in a still more highly attenuate and subtle form into its very substance, first into the cortical substance, next into the medullary, in which latter, therefore, we see the most manifest signs of the ramification of membranes. And inasmuch as similar substances are found in nearly every part of the cerebrum, and also of the cerebellum, and in the medulla oblongata throughout, so we conclude that the soul resides particularly in the cortical substance of the cerebrum, and partly also in the medullary, where these exquisitely subtle membranes, from the structure of the organ, can run connectedly from particle to particle, and likewise above, around and within every particle of the above substance. [34]

A manuscript also dated during this period (generally assumed to have been written between January and February 1734)[35] contains among other things some observations and notes[36] by Swedenborg with reference to Christian Wolff's *Psychologia Empirica* which was published towards the end of 1732.[37] Swedenborg had clearly read Wolff extensively[38] and references (as well as explicit quotations) from the works of the German philosopher appear frequently in his works. In general we see Swedenborg adopting Wolff's[39] views with regard to the analysis of the various faculties of the soul, which he defines and classifies in a substantially analogous way to Wolff's *Psychologia Empirica*.

Swedenborg's reasons for seeking an explanation for the movements of the soul however—based on exclusively physiological foundations—are different, and worth detailing. It is worth noticing, in particular, the attention given to an explanation of complex activities such as perception, intellect, reflection and will, which are described as intelligible processes starting from the physical conditions of the membranes of the nervous system.[40] As stated above, for Swedenborg, the soul is a material structure of which he is convinced, one day, of the possibility *si microscopium haberemus,* [being made accessible by a microscope] to examine *totam structuram tam animam quam spiritum* [its entire structure so far as its life and spirit].[41] Swedenborg re-affirms the idea that guided him in the *Principia*; that there is a single nature that is governed by a single general law and that all the organic and inorganic realities that belong to the world of finite entities constitute a mechanically regulated order. In this way, the law of the spiral movement derived from the *conatus* of the metaphysical point becomes the law of the soul as well. Therefore the soul must not be thought of as an entity that requires a different metaphysical *status*, but rather as a substance that is structurally tied to the body, sharing its nature and therefore showing a natural harmony and correspondence with it.

These observations obviously move Swedenborg's viewpoint away from that of Wolff. Wolff begins from a roughly Cartesian position,[42] and asserts that the soul is a substance different to, and distinct from, the body.[43] For Wolff the soul is an *ens simplex* [a simple, or singular substance] devoid of movement, but with a *vis* [power] consisting in a *continuo agendi conatu* [a force that is continually active].[44] For Swedenborg, as we have seen, the soul is not an *ens simplex* but rather a compound of active and finite entities. For this reason it constitutes a mechanism that is certainly perfect and refined, but can be explained in an absolutely natural way. In this way he seems closer to Leibniz than to Wolff, particularly when Leibniz is critical of Cartesian dualism and asserts a metaphysical monism that identifies the monad as the real foundation (both of the extended and the non extended). In a substantially analogous way, Swedenborg will be led to derive reality—in all its finite determinations—from a single *ens* [substance], the metaphysical or natural point.

These differences are evidenced even more clearly in a later publication, usually dated around 1742[45] (written, therefore, after the publication of the *Oeconomia Regni Animalis* [*Economy of the Animal Kingdom*]).[46] In this manuscript Swedenborg moves even further from Wolff's tenets and criticises, in particular, the foundations of Wolff's psychology: according to which the essence of the soul consists in an innate force which is a representation of the universe. Swedenborg's objection was that it remained totally incomprehensible how a representation of something could be possible without some form of mediation between the representation itself and the represented object. Once a dichotomous relationship between entities is recognised, it becomes inexplicable for Swedenborg how a force (the soul) can represent another entity (the body) to itself without there being some connection and link that permits us to understand the action of such a force. If it is impossible for a force acting in a void to move bodies, it is also impossible, in the same way, for the *vis insita animae* [power implanted in the soul] to represent: '*universi situ corporis organici in universo materialiter et constitutione organorum sensorium formaliter limitata*' [the general organic and material body which constitutes the formal limits of the sense organs][47] unless the representations and perceptions are already innate in the soul.[48] The alternative is to admit to hidden and therefore totally incomprehensible qualities[49] governing this force.

By far the biggest disagreement however—or the one that Swedenborg expresses most clearly—concerns the workings of the harmony between body and soul itself. Wolff is absolutely convinced of the existence of this harmony, and gives ample demonstrations in both his *Psychologia Empirica* and his *Psychologia Rationalis*. In reality, Swedenborg rather slavishly follows the order of presentation of the solutions given to the problems of the third section of the *Psychologia Rationalis* which presents, in succession, the theories of physical influx, occasional influx and pre-determined harmony.[50] With reference to this latter position, Swedenborg presents a series of critical considerations that will push him to specify his own argument on this question. In fact he maintains, once again, that the system of pre-determined harmony involves the *a priori* acceptance of the impossibility of understanding the manner in which this harmony itself is achieved. As such it leaves the problem of the interaction of body and soul in total obscurity. On the other hand, Wolff himself had admitted that '*In systemate harmoniae praestabilitae mechanismus corporis est nobis incomprensibilis non tamen probabilitate destituitur*' [In the system belonging to the pre-established harmony, the mechanisms of the harmony are beyond our comprehension, though not beyond the bounds of possibility].[51]

For his part, Swedenborg proposes a solution centred on the hypothesis of a relationship or a *commercium* between body and soul. They have a natural correspondence and connection that is justified on the basis of a common origin—or of a similar material constitution—which renders them subject to the same mechanism and laws. In the *De Anima* [*The Soul* or *Rational Psychology*], dated 1742, he clarifies what he means by *correspondentia* with an example derived from the process of verbal communication that involves perception, mental representation of objects and the expression of ideas represented through language.[52] Swedenborg affirms that the description of a house, field, painting or any other object through language produces the idea of these objects immediately and without difficulty. Yet words are really nothing but 'tremulations' and vibrations, movements that are produced in the vocal organs, spread into the environment and can reach the sense organs and the membranes of a recipient and be transformed into images or ideas in the soul. The linguistic relationship between the word, which certainly has a physical substratum and its meaning is introduced by Swedenborg to account for that complex system of relationships and interactions which he assumes must exist between body and soul. This is a natural relationship and is therefore different from that of the pre-determined harmony. The movements of the body and workings of the soul therefore, correspond perfectly and make up different functions of a single natural process that involves the communication between entities on the basis of a single order that links together the determinations of the finite and connects them to the first *ens* from which everything derives.

In summary therefore, these are some of the elements that emerge from a first approach to the texts dedicated by Swedenborg to an analysis of the body and soul relationship. It is one of the central themes in his work as a natural philosopher, but it returns as a frequent motif in the later visionary works. It is curious that in *De Commercio Animae et Corporis* [*The Interaction of the Soul and Body*], a later work belonging to his old age, he highlights the relationship between body and soul while describing one of his celestial visions. He makes it the subject of a discussion between supporters of Aristotle, Descartes and Leibniz, engaged in expounding their respective ideas. At the end of the discussion, the philosophers find their ideas extremely confused and abandon all definitions of the question, leaving it to a random drawing to decide on the matter. Perhaps this conclusion aims at showing that such investigation could not be completed even in the heavens. As seeker of truth, however, man still has to undertake the task, pursue it, and ceaselessly investigate the different facets of natural and spiritual reality.

Notes

[1] For an understanding of my previous research into Swedenborg, please see my *La filosofia della natura di Emanuel Swedenborg*, [Emanuel Swedenborg's Philosophy of Nature] Franco Angeli, Milan, 1999.

[2] One of my first works on the body-soul relationship in Swedenborg is *Per un'anatomia dell'anima: Emanuel Swedenborg Versus Christian Wolff*, [An Anatomy of the Soul: Emanuel Swedenborg Versus Christian Wolff] in AA VV, *Ragione, natura, storia. Quattro studi sul Settecento*, [Reason, Nature, History: Four Studies on the 18th Century] Franco Angeli, Milan, 1999, pp.13-38.

[3] For an overview of the theme please see: D M Armstrong, *Recent Work on Relation of Mind and Brain*, in G Fløistad, (ed. by), *Contemporary Philosophy: a New Survey*, Nijhoff, The Hague 1982, vol. III, pp. 45-79; P Smith, O R Jones, *The Philosophy of Mind. An Introduction*, CUP, Cambridge 1986; S Moravia, *L'enigma della mente*, [The Enigma of the Mind] Laterza, Roma-Bari 1986; H Gardner, *The Mind's New Science. A History of the Cognitive Revolution*, Basic Books, New York 1985, Italian transl., *La nuova scienza della mente. Storia della rivoluzione cognitiva*, Feltrinelli, Milan 1988; C McDonald, *Mind-Body Identity Theories*, Routledge, London 1989; W Bechtel, *Philosophy of Mind. An Overview for Cognitive Science*, Laurence Erlbaum Associates Inc., Hillsdale 1988, Italian translation *Filosofia della mente*, Il Mulino, Bologna 1992; G Strawson, *Mental Reality*, The MIT Press, Cambridge (Mass.) 1994; J L Bermudez, A Marcel, N Eilan, *The Body and the Self*, Brandford Book, MIT Press, Cambridge (Mass.) 1998. Cf. M Di Francesco, *Introduzione alla filosofia della mente*, [Introduction to the Philosophy of Mind] La Nuova Italia Scientifica, Roma 1996, p. 15. See also by the same author *L'io e i suoi sé. Identità personale e scienza della mente*, [The Self and its Selves.

Personal Identity and Science of the Mind] R Cortina Editor, Milan 1998. We shall restrict ourselves to giving some titles that show the great interest that contemporary historians have in these themes: J W Yolton, *Thinking Matter, Materialism in Eighteenth-Century Britain*, University of Minnesota Press, Minneapolis 1983, repr. 1984; S Landucci, *Mente e corpo nel dibattito fra Collins e Clarke*, [Mind and Body in the Collins and Clarke Debate] in A Santucci (Ed.) *L'età dei Lumi. Saggi sulla cultura settecentesca*, [The Age of Enlightenment. Essays on Eighteenth Century Culture] Il Mulino, Bologna 1998, pp. 125-142; J P Wright, *Materialismo e anima vitale alla metà del XVIII secolo. Il pensiero medico, Ibid.*, [Materialism and Life Soul in the Mid-18th Century Medical Thought] pp. 143-157, L Turco, *Mente e corpo nel 'Trattato' di Hume. Problemi storiografici, Ibid.*, [Mind and Body in Hume's 'Treatise'. Historiographical Problems] pp. 159-187, see also the more general historical reconstruction given in *The Cambridge History of Seventeenth-Century Philosophy*, ed. by D Garber, M Ayers, CUP, Cambridge, 1998, vol. I chaps. IV-V.

[4] Cf. E Swedenborg, *De Commercio Animae et Corporis*, London, 1769, transl. by G Dole, *Soul-Body Interaction*, in *The Universal Human and Soul-Body Interactions*, Paulist Press, New York 1984. This treatise has also been translated into Italian by L Scocia, titled: *Sul commercio dell'anima e del corpo che credersi esistere o per influsso fisico, o per influsso spirituale o per armonia prestabilita*, M Ricci, Firenze 1885.

[5] The work is published in three volumes. Here we are only interested in the first volume, *Principia Rerum Naturalium sive Novorum Tentaminum Phaenomena Mundi Elementaris Philosophice Explicandi*, Friderici Hekelii, Dresdae et Lipsiae 1734. Quotations from Swedenborg's texts maintain the original spelling and italics.

[6] Cf. *Anatomi af vär aldrafinaste natur, wisande att wärt rorande och lefwande wäsende består af contremiscientier*. See the English translation of this text by C Th Odhner, *On Tremulation*, Boston 1899, repr. Swedenborg Scientific Association, Bryn Athyn, PA 1976, which we refer to.

[7] Cf. E Swedenborg, *On Trem...*, cit., p. 14.

[8] Cf. *The Letters and Memorials of Emanuel Swedenborg*, transl. and ed. by A Acton, 2 voll., Swedenborg Scientific Association, Bryn Athyn, PA 1948, vol. I, p. 228.

[9] Cf. E Swedenborg, *Principia Rerum Naturalium,...*, cit., vol. I, Pars I, p. 6.

[10] The text of *Mechanismo Animae et Corporis* is contained in the third of the ten volumes of the *Photolithographs Manuscripts*, (Codex 88, pp. 116-131), edited by R L Tafel in Stockholm, in 1869-70. The manuscript was translated by A Stroh in 1905, now in *Scientific and Philosophical Treatises (1716-1740) by Emanuel Swedenborg*, 2nd ed. by W R Woofenden, Swedenborg Scientific Association, Bryn Athyn, PA 1992, pp. 123-146.

[11] Cf. E Swedenborg, *On the Mechanism...*, cit., pp. 123-124.

[12] Cf. E Swedenborg, *On the Mechanism...*, cit., p. 129.

[13] Cf. E Swedenborg, *On the Mechanism...*, p. 129.

[14] Cf. Ibid., p. 138.

[15] Cf. Ibid., pp. 139-140.

[16] Between 1743 and 1744, Swedenborg carried out anatomical research on the brain, translated and edited by R L Tafel, *The Brain, Considered Anatomically, Physiologically and Philosophically*, vol. 1, The Swedenborg Society, London 1882, repr. I 1934, vol. 2, J Speirs, London 1887.

[17] Cf. E Swedenborg, *On the Mechanism* p. 140.

[18] Cf. E Swedenborg, *On the Mechanism*..., cit., pp. 131-132. Swedenborg says that animals' souls are made from cruder membranes (Cf. Ibid., p. 130) and die, even if not immediately (Cf. *Ibid.*, p. 132). Of the human soul Swedenborg writes: 'When man dies the soul lives because it cannot perish, since it consists in such a subtle part, which cannot putrefy, nor perish from fire, nor air, nor otherwise; therefore it remains'. Cf. Ibid, pp. 145-146.

[19] Cf. E Swedenborg, *On the Mechanism...*, cit,. pp. 133-134

[20] Cf. *Prodromus Philosophiae Ratiocinantis de Infinito, et Causa Finali Creationis: deque Mechanismo operationis Animae et Corporis*, sumptibus Friderici Hekelii, Dresdae et Lipsiae 1734, repr.. Tho. Murray Gorman, Kegan Paul, Trench, et Soc., Londini 1836, which we used, but see also the English translation *Forerunner of a Reasoned Philosophy Concerning the Infinite, the Final Cause of Creation also the Mechanism of the Operation of the Soul and Body* by J J Garth Wilkinson with an introduction by L F Hite, The Swedenborg Society, London 1902, repr. 1908, 1915.

[21] Cf. E Swedenborg, *Prodromus*..., cit., pp. 165-166.

[22] With reference to this: '...ex his et aliis perplurimis argumentis concludi potest, nihil dari in rerum natura, quatenus est infinita, et qualitates et modos habet, quod non suis regulis gaudeat; pariter quod in nostris naturalibus nullae aliae regulae dentur, quam geometricae et mechanicae'. Cf. *Prodromus*..., cit., p. 178.

[23] It is interesting to note that with reference to this context Swedenborg in his *The Way to a Knowledge of the Soul*, (cit., p. 159), makes direct reference to the *De Bombyce* of Marcello Malpighi, who writes: 'Cum enim tota in minimis existat natura, si alicubi, magis equidem in insectorum moleculis id deprehendi par fuerit'. Cf. M Malpighi, *De Bombyce*, apud J Martyn & J Allestry, Londini 1669, p. 1. Malpighi is one of the many authors quoted by Swedenborg in his anatomical works and who deserve a more thorough evaluation.

[24] Cf. E Swedenborg, *Prodromus*..., cit., pp. 263-264.

[25] Cf. E Swedenborg, *The Infinite*..., cit., pp158-159

[26] Cf. E Swedenborg, *Prodromus*..., cit., p. 189 sgg.

[27] Cf. E Swedenborg, *Prodromus*..., cit., p. 190.

[28] Cf. E Swedenborg, *Prodromus*..., cit., p. 189.

[29] Cf. E Swedenborg, *Prodromus*..., cit., pp. 191-192.

[30] Swedenborg says that some philosophers considered the soul as something unknown but

still wanted to: '...nexum ejus cum corpore jam hoc jam alio modo remonstrare: quum enim de ignoto agitur, quod non volumus tanquam simile cum notis agnoscere, non potest aliud inde existere, quam ut inde formatae sententiae et conclusiones emanent, quae tamen nihil demostrant; hinc maxima pars in spiritus animales juraverant, et omnes motus per illos tandem explicuerat, tamen ita ut juberet anima, et illi jussa exequerentur, et jam irent ad has partes, jam vero ad illas, et functiones reginae suae ut famuli peragerent'. Cf. *Prodromus...*, cit., p. 198.

[31] Cf. E Swedenborg, *The Infinite...*, cit., p.175

[32] Swedenborg explains this concept very clearly: 'Primum occurrit, quod generaliter hic possim tradere, quod omnis nexus supponat contiguum, et quod sine contiguo nullus nexus concipi aut dari possit; si nexus sit, erunt fines, si fines, erunt media; et nisi fines per media connexi sint, nullus datur nexus: in mechanicis substantialibus hoc notissimum est, quod scilicet nullus nexus concipi posst sine contiguo: in natura invisibili, in qua apparet nexus cum visibili, supponitur omnino contiguum, ut una pars tangat vel moveat alteram ab uno fine ad alterum: materialiter connexum seu qua motum connexum, non potest aliter percipi, si velimus secundum rationem loqui, quam ut sint media ordine et successive connexam per quae se respiciant fines'. Cf. *Prodromus...*, cit., pp. 211-212.

[33] In the *Prodromus* we read: '...sine mediis illis foret anima destituta sua vi et facultate operandi, destituta sentiendi illa, quae in crassioribus peraguntur; destituta facultate una cum corpore operandi, destituta in motum ciendi similia et hoc distinctius et distinctius; verbo foret anima sine corpore, et corpus sine anima sensibili in corpore: si ipsae mediae membranae amitterent vel suum nexum, vel tonum vel tensionem, illico quid dissimile contra usum et cultum repraesentaretur animae; quumque operari incipit, per turbam dissimilium operari debet, adeo ut nihil rationale prodire possit; unde omne rationale non est solius animae, sed etiam reliquarum partium in nexu et contiguo a sensibus usque ad animam'. Cf. *Prodromus...*, cit., p. 256.

[34] Cf. E Swedenborg, *The Infinite...*, cit., pp.222-23.

[35] Cf. A Acton, *Phychologica Being Notes and Observations on Christian Wolf's Psychologia Empirica by Emanuel Swedenborg*, Swedenborg Scientific Association, Philadelphia, PA 1923, p. xii.

[36] The codex is identified with the number 88, and the notes we refer to here are in pages 159-213. Later reproduced in *Swedenborg Photolithographed Manuscripts* (pp. 159-206), these pages were originally untitled, now go under the title *Phychologica*, in the collection edited by A Acton in 1923, Cf. *op. cit.*

[37] C G Ludovici gives a timely notice of the dating of Wolff's works, published in Frankfurt and Leipzig in *Historie des Wolffischen Philosophie*, [History of Wolff's Philosophy] Leipzig 1738, p. 67. The text of *Psychologia Empirica, methodo scientifica pertractata, qua ea, quae De Anima Humana indubia experientiae fide constant, continentur et ad Solidam*

Universae Philosophiae Praticae ac Theologiae Naturalis Tractationem via Sternitur Abt. II, Lateinische Schriften, [Latin writings] 5. Bd., Olms, Hildesheim 1968, that we refer to has now appeared in the edition of the *Opera Omnia* of Chr. Wolff, *Gesammelte Werke, Materialien und Dokumente* [Collected Works, Materials and Documents] edited by J Ecole, M Thomann, H W Arndt, 59 voll., Olms, Hildesheim-New York 1965-ss.

[38] There was an edition of the *Cosmologia Generalis* in Swedenborg's library cf. *Swedenborg's Library, an Alphabetical List*, 'The New Philosophy', LXXII, 1, 1969, pp. 115-126. Swedenborg also directly refers to Wolff's *Ontologia* and *Cosmologia* in the same codex 88. The text of the brief annotation *Comparatio Onthologiae et Cosmologiae generalis Dni. Christiani Wolfii Cum Principiis nostris rerum naturalium*, is available in *Emanuel Swedenborg Opera Quaedam, aut inedita aut obsoleta de rebus naturalibus, introductionem adiunxit Svante Arrhenius, edidit Alfred H Stroh, ex officina Aftonbladet*, Holmiae 3 voll., *Cosmologica*, vol. III, p. 197. Furthermore, in 1734, Swedenborg states that he found confirmation of his own system in Wolff's *Ontologia* and *Cosmologia* di Wolff, (cf. *Principia*..., cit., pp. 451-452). In the first volume of *Elementa Matheseos Universae*, (I. Bd., §46) Wolff quotes Swedenborg directly in a memoire entitled *De novo calcolo sexagenario, qui a beatae memoriae rege Sueciae Carolo XII adiventus est*, published by Swedenborg in *Miscellanea Observata circa res naturales et praesertim circa mineralia, ignem et montium strata*, Pars IV, vulgo Schiffbeck bey Hamburg, typis Herm. Heinr. Holli, Naupotami 1722.

[39] Cf. E Swedenborg, *Comparatio*..., cit., p. 197. The spread of Wolff's thought in Sweden has been studied by T Frängsmyr in *Wolffianismens genombrott i Uppsala. Frihetsida universitetsfilosofi till 1700-talets mitt*, Acta Universitatis Upsaliensis, Uppsala 1972, although no mention of Swedenborg is made. K P Nemitz gives a passing hint of Swedenborg's references to Wolff, in *The German Philosophers Leibniz and Wolff in Swedenborg's Philosophic Development*, 'The New Philosophy', XCVII, 3-4, 1994, pp. 411-425; see also, *Christian Wolff & Swedenborg*, 'The New Philosophy', CII, 1-2, 1999, pp. 391-412 by the same author.

[40] Cf. E Swedenborg, *Psychologica*..., cit., pp. 110-115.

[41] Cf. E Swedenborg, *Psychologica*..., cit., p. 79.

[42] In *Psychologia Rationalis*, first published in 1734, the year of the publication of Swedenborg's *Principia* Wolff writes: 'Recte omnia sese habent, sed ostendendumerat, modificationes animae non esse explicabiles per eadem principia, per quae explicantur modificationes corporis: quod magis sumere, quam probare videtur *Cartesius* nos vero in superioribus evicimus (§44, §46), ut adeo nostra de anima philosophia *Cartesianam* non subvertat, sed eandem illustret et corroboret'. Cf. *op. cit.*, II. Abt. Lateinische Schriften, 6. Bd., §51, p. 34. For Wolff's psychology see M Campo, *Cristiano Wolff e il razionalismo precritico*, 2 voll., Vita e Pensiero, Milano 1939, repr.. Olms, Hildesheim-New York 1980, J Ecole, *La métaphysique de Christian Wolff*, Olms, Hildesheim 1990, the *Introductio* by the same writer as the *Psychologia empirica*, pp. IV-XX, the miscellaneous volume *Nuovi studi sul pensiero*

di Christian Wolff, edited by S Carboncini and L Cataldi Madonna, 'Il Cannocchiale', 2-3, 1989, repr. G Olms, Hildesheim 1992, see also R G Blackwell, *Christian Wolff's Doctrine of the Soul*, 'Journal of the History of Ideas', XXII, 3, 1961, pp. 339-354; di A M Vitadello, *Experience et raison dans la psychologie de Christian Wolff*, 'Revue Philosophique de Louvain', 71, 1973, pp. 488-510; by C A Körr, *Christian Wolff's Distinction between Empirical and Rational Psychology*, 'Studia Leibnitiana Supplementa', B. XIV, 1975, Id., *Cartesian Themes in Wolff's German Metaphysics*, in W Scheinders (hg.), *Christian Wolff 1679-1754*, F Meiner, Hamburg 1983, by P Pimpinella, *Spiritus nella Psychologia Rationalis di Christian Wolff*, [Spiritus in Christian Wolff's Psychologia Rationalis] in *Spiritus*, IV Coll. Int. (Roma, 7-9 genn. 1983), edited by M Fattori and M Bianchi, Editori dell' Roma, 1984, pp. 429-447, by V Gessa-Kurotschka, *Il desiderio del bene. Sulle origini* etc,. *The desire For Good. For the Origins of Modern Practical Philosophy in Germany* see, Guerini, Milano 1996, in particular chaps. I, III.

[43] Cf. Chr Wolff, *Psychologia Rationalis...*, cit., §52, p. 35.

[44] Cf. Chr Wolff, *Psycologia Rationalis...*, cit., §54, p. 35.

[45] The text of the manuscript contained in Codex 74, was translated into English and published in 1920 by A Acton, with the title *The Soul and the Harmony between Soul and Body*, in a miscellany titled *Psychological Transactions and Other Posthumous Tracts 1734-1744*, which is now available in an edition corrected by the Swedenborg Scientific Association, Bryn Athyn, PA 1984, pp. 23-64 which we shall use for references.

[46] The *Oeconomia* was published anonymously in two volumes, respectively: *Oeconomia regni animalis in transactiones divisa: quarum haec prima, de sanguine, ejus arteriis, venis, et corde agit: anatomice, physice, et philosophice perlustrata. Cui accedit Introductio ad Psychologiam rationalem*. Impensis auctoris, venditur Londini et Amstelodami, apud F Changuion, 1740, and *Oeconomia regni animalis in transactiones divisa: quarum haec secunda de cerebri motu et cortice, et de anima humana agit: anatomice, physice, et philosophice perlustrata*, F Changuion, Amstelodami 1741. This work was translated into English with the title *The Economy of Animal Kingdom, Considered Anatomically, Physically, and Philosophically*, A Clissold, ed., 2 vol., W Newbery, H Balliere, London 1845, Otis Clapp, Boston 1846 reprinted in 1903 and 1955. The *Oeconomia*, alongside a large part of Swedenborg's anatomical and physiological work still has not been studied systematically. It should be borne in mind that in 1744-45, Swedenborg printed *Regnum animale, anatomice, physice, et philosophice perlustratum*, translated into English with the title *The Animal Kingdom, Considered Anatomically, Physically, and Philosophically*, 2 vol., ed J J G Wilkinson, W Newbery, London 1843-44, reprinted by the London Swedenborg Scientific Society in 1960.

[47] Cf. Chr Wolff, *Psychologia Rationalis...*, cit., §66, p.45.

[48] Cf. E Swedenborg, *Psychologica...*, cit., p. 36. With reference to this, Swedenborg adds that the soul would behave as if in a kind of mirror that limits itself to reflecting the objects in the universe passively. Cf. Ibid., p. 35.

[49] Swedenborg makes many references to the danger of reintroducing hidden qualities. Cf. Ibid., pp. 34, 36.

[50] Cf. C Wolff, *Psychologia Rationalis...*, cit., respectively: section III, chap. II, pp. 480-512; chap. III, pp. 513-541; chap. IV, pp. 542-587.

[51] Cf. C Wolff, *Psychologia Rationalis...*, cit., §637, p. 577.

[52] Cf. E Swedenborg, *De Anima...*, cit., p. 76.

Swedenborg and the Comparative Philosophy of the Soul

Michael Costello

Though physicalism is the current dominant doctrine, many philosophers and scientists still hold that in personal experience, (i.e. in the accounts that other humans give of themselves and through animal behaviour), there are features which cannot be explained by the laws of physics. A current and commonly used all-inclusive term for such features is mind. Earlier philosophies used the term soul (*anima*, *psyche*).

One problem with any account of Swedenborg's view on the soul is that it is closely bound up with his difficult notion of degrees. Such are the cross connections between them that it is hard to expound them separately or to know where to begin. Here I have opted to emphasise certain leading aspects of the soul with no more than unavoidable allusions to the theory of degrees, whose very definition is uncertain.[1] One possible approach to degrees is through the distinction by Plato[2] and Aristotle[3] of reason and the senses, as higher and lower parts of the soul which fit into a scheme, which is, or may be similar to that of biological levels of organisation, such as we find applied to psychology by modern authors like N Tinbergen (*The Study of Instinct*) and Arthur Koestler (*Act of Creation*).[4] Few western authors have remained untouched by the Platonic/Aristotelian distinction of sense and reason. But Swedenborg adds a third 'internal' level of function on top of these which is unknown to western thought but familiar to Indian and Chinese thought and which he describes in *Arcana Caelestia*[5] and *Rational Psychology* as above ordinary consciousness. Somewhat confusingly he uses the term soul only for this highest level in *Rational Psychology*. Rather than adding a level, Swedenborg's near contemporaries often subtracted a level, collapsing reason and sense into one, reducing thought to associations in the imagination.[6] This notion is still current.[7]

I have singled out four important aspects of the soul: sensation; consciousness; the self; and multiple souls. My reason for selecting the first two is that they are the grounds most commonly used by modern authors for distinguishing between soul and body (rather than life or reason).[8] The reason for discussing the self is that it bridges the ages of discussion about the soul from the most ancient and mythological to modern times—no mean virtue in a context where it is difficult to be sure that authors from different times (or even the same time), though they use the same terms, mean the same thing. I close on the concept of multiple souls because although somewhat lacking in European thought as it was rejected by Thomas Aquinas and Descartes, and hard to reconcile with the concept of soul as self, it is prominent in non-European cultures and is in some way related to the doctrine of degrees.

These four topics stand in different relation to Swedenborg's ideas. As for sense-data and consciousness, the ideas of Swedenborg's contempories were somewhat misty compared with later times. Neither of these notions were at the forefront of Swedenborg's attention, though he does articulate the notion of consciousness and the more unusual idea of multiple fields of consciousness in one body.[9] The case with the self is different. It was at the forefront of Swedenborg's attention, and Locke and Hume brought it to the attention of philosophy. The notion of multiple souls in one body is somewhat alien to European Philosophy, but widespread in ancient and other cultures. It is related to multiple fields of consciousness for after Descartes a generally held assumption has emerged that a soul is conscious. It is related in some instances to Swedenborg's concept of degrees (spanning both the early and late periods of his thought,) and also to his concept of a communion with spirits. Multiple fields of consciousness did, after Swedenborg's time, come under discussion in Europe in relation to the unconscious, hypnotic dissociation, and Morton Prince's study of multiple personality. That is more like the communion of spirits rather than degrees of consciousness. I will now move on to discuss each of these topics in more detail, and seperately, despite some overlap.

Sensation

The basis for a now common argument for the existence of something non-physical is found (paradoxically) in the arch materialist Democritus (460-370 BC). According to Democritus,[10] the world consists of empty space filled with atoms. Atoms have only motion, shape, size and hardness. Colour, sound, smell, heat and cold are left out in the cold by this—they are sensed but the senses only provide appearances, as evidenced by the fact that we don't sense atoms.

This view was later taken up by Galileo (1564-1642) and by another materialist Thomas Hobbes (1588-1679).[11] Hobbes was able to ignore the implied non-materiality of sensory events by calling them phantasms. But we can't get rid of them by being rude to them as C D Broad points out.[12] John Locke (1632-1704) (Hobbes' younger and Swedenborg's older contemporary) introduced the term 'idea' and 'idea of sensation' to stand for sensory appearances[13] (the precursor of the later terms 'sense data',[14] 'sensa'[15] and 'qualia'). By Locke's time the world-picture of Democritus had become the world-picture of scientists, such as Robert Boyle (1627-91) and Isaac Newton (1642-1727). Locke nevertheless points out that the ideas of sensation have not only supposedly illusory properties like colour that are banished from the 'scientific' world, but also properties like those the scientists credit material objects with: shape, hardness, motion, number and time. Locke terms the properties of sensation resembling those studied by physicists 'primary' qualities. He calls 'secondary' those non-Democritian qualities like colour and smell that may be attributed to the material world by non-scientists (though T Reid (1710-96) says the non-scientist also recognises the subjective character of secondary qualities).[16] Thus we see in the sense object, the 'appearance' of Democritus, combination of matter-like primary qualities and non-matter-like secondary qualities. The latter, at least, are non-material and therefore if the soul is defined as something non-material associated with the body, the soul exists.

Even today, it could be said, such an argument stands up. Any physics textbook will show the three dimensions of mass, length and time as fundamental (method of dimensions), seemingly agreeing with Democritus, Newton and Locke. And even though the underlying conception of these quantities is altogether changed because of relativity and quantum physics, it has not changed in a way that could explain sense data.[17] Hence the argument for an immaterial factor still stands. But are these 'sense data' or 'sensa' what we usually mean by mind or soul? After all, they appear spatially extended and, with 'sensa', what appears *is*. Traditionally understood, at least after Rene Descartes, philosophy has held a view of the soul as non-extended.[18] At the very least it seems the present line of thought gives rise to questions about the status of sense objects. One response is to argue that sensa are a third type of object, neither mental or material, a view which has been named *trialism*. Another is that they are simply mental, which according to George Berkeley (1685-1753), means that experiences such as intense heat or warmth etc, are simply feeling, and he would extend this conclusion to all other aspects of sensation.[19]

Professor Maria Crasta has previously highlighted the textual evidence that, in his scientific period, Swedenborg was a materialist,[20] and his views on sensation were very different from the above. He identified sensation with the activity of the cortical cells and even understanding with the activity of the 'simple cortex' (a hypothetical part of the cortex postulated by Swedenborg but not recognised by modern science).[21] He also denies that there are sensation and rationality after death.[22] He does however attribute survival to the supra-intellectual soul[23] which I think is identical with the internal man described in *Arcana Caelestia*.[24] In *Rational Psychology*[25] he also links this with the view that the highest parts of the nervous system are the last to perish. (This is quite contrary to subsequent science which has shown that the lowest parts of the nervous system are the least delicate. Witness the activity of headless chickens and cockroaches and the amusement of the 'dancing dead man' which involves getting a recent corpse to move by setting it on fire, an entertainment of the recent Afghan war according to *The Guardian*). It is obvious in Swedenborg's later, theological writings, that his earlier materialism has changed, for spirits are said to have sensation,[26] when yet the brain with its cortex (in his earlier view, the organ of sensation) has been destroyed in death. He also states that spirits are not in space or time but in appearances of these.[27] Yet there is an odd passage in *Arcana Caelestia* at §444-46, where he insists on the soul being extended. He speaks of the subject and object of thought as extended. One might conjecture that this had something to do with the extension of sensa (see above). Alternatively the passage might be thought of as a vestige of his earlier materialism. I have no satisfactory explanation, but the problem is worth mentioning.

Now Swedenborg also says that the spirits of the dead not only have emotion, reason and memory but also exquisite sensations and apparent bodies. He says that man lives as a man after death and it seems that the (apparent) body is involved in his concept of a man as with Thomas Aquinas and Aristotle, who however, denied that man lived as man after death saying that he lived as emotionless reason (Aristotle), or that he did not live as a man until the general resurrection (Aquinas).

But Swedenborg goes on to emphasise that the apparent body lives in an apparent environment of objects similar to those in the present life. In this he agrees with the traditional African view of the spiritual world as given by Mbiti.[28] But what are these objects? It is tempting to identify them with sensa. But I know of no passage where he defines the status of these spiritual objects in a way that I might understand. I think it is best to be cautious about attributing to him any version of sensum theory such as outlined above.

But even though sensum theory——a theory of sensation stemming from Democritus—— may be foreign to Swedenborg, it certainly gives support to some of Swedenborg's positions.

First of all let us take the Swedenborgian position that man survives death.[29] If man were solely the body (the atoms of the elements in a particular spatial arrangement), it would hardly seem possible that we would survive death. For we can observe the body's decomposition.[30] If on the other hand there is something immaterial (such as sensation) it is not clear what will happen to it. But perhaps we can go even further, and taking the maxim *in nihilo nihil fit*, state that the power of sensing cannot just disappear.[31] One option is that it might lie dormant, so I think we do not have here a complete argument for immortality, but certainly one which brings it out of the region of near impossibility. This kind of argument also entails some form of survival for animals, as Leibniz observed, though this does not seem to have attracted comment from Swedenborg who indeed had originally denied that even the human power of sensation survived death.[32] It is part of the argument that the soul survives to the point that it is in some way simple, that is consciousness (see below), which embraces the sensations, does not consist of particles that can be divided. The soul's simplicity was denied by Hume, in particular, and his view is shared by the younger George Berkeley[33] and Buddhism.[34] More surprisingly Swedenborg in his earlier phase and perhaps even in his later work does not acknowledge the soul as simple.

Secondly, let us look at the position that man senses objects after death.[35] According to sense datum theory, the objects sensed in this life are in themselves immaterial (even though caused by material objects in most accounts, although not according to Berkeley and Leibniz). Therefore there seems to be much less difficulty in accounting for sense perception in the next life. For according to Democritus/Locke, the clothes that ones sees or feels on a person are just as ghostly as any worn by a spirit, even though caused by material clothes which cannot be directly felt by the senses, but only inferred. This surely makes Swedenborg's account of the other life more plausible than the naive view that we see matter directly. [36]

Consciousness

The concept of consciousness (or awareness) is notoriously difficult to define. In life we have a series of brief conscious fields—which are not instantaneous,[37] or else we would not see movement or experience change. By field is meant that we are conscious of several objects together including consciousness itself. We remember conscious fields, or aspects of them from different times, and we recall bits of them. One common confusion is to equate sleep with unconsciousness but the Edinburgh researchers [38] have shown that people woken during sleep are able to offer an account of their state if asked quickly enough (and not only during REM but at any time during sleep). Such research appears to vindicate Descartes—who maintained the soul was always conscious—against Locke who maintained it was not in sleep.[39] Finally it may be mentioned that the distinction of consciousness from the properties of matter leads to the same arguments for a non-physical or psi factor as did the secondary qualities in the section above.

The word consciousness appears in Swedenborg's works, as does the term sensation (feeling) in the sense used by later authors. Perception is another synonym for consciousness (as in Berkeley's *esse est percipi*), but Swedenborg uses perception in an unusual sense meaning intuitive judgement (i.e. 'Perception consists in seeing what is true and what is false').[40] Yet he also states that perception has a close relationship to sensation, saying that perception is internal sensation and vice versa.[41]

At §171 of *Rational Psychology* he distinguishes processes in the body of which we are and are not conscious. 'When there is no proceeding rational will' he states, 'as in the case in the cerebellum, and the cerebrum itself during sleep...the human intellect is not rendered conscious of its operations'. We may hesitate to accept this about the sleeping cerebrum because of the Edinburgh work[42] but his meaning is clear. So too at §38, where he states, 'we are not conscious of any other changes save as they affect the cortex of the cerebrum', which is a very modern view and perfectly clear. Clear also is the acount at *Arcana Caelestia* §4622; 'It is not the body which sees, hears, smells and feels but its spirit'.[43] For the term 'spirit' today we would now use 'mind' (as already stated). Consciousness is mental rather than physical, bodily, or material just as the secondary qualities (see above) are not physical, bodily or material.

Likewise, there are other statements by Swedenborg which relate the notion of consciousness to that of the internal man in *Arcana Caelestia* (if, as I presume, this equals the *anima* as described in *Rational Psychology*). Now, to me, Swedenborg's definition of the internal man is 'X', a complete unknown (similar to the *atman* of Indian psychology and the *hun* of Chinese (see below)). However, his statements are very promising for study as they may provide some guidance as to how to arrive at knowledge of this internal. I shall therefore cite some of them. On consciousness, the *anima* and pure intellect. *Rational Psychology* at §8 ends 'the soul is the only substance in the body that sensates, since it is the only substance that purely understands what is sensated'. This sounds almost the same as *Arcana Caelestia* §4622 but is in fact quite different as *spiritus* in *Arcana Caelestia* means the whole mind and the *anima* in *Rational Psychology* refers only to the highest part. And elsewhere in the same, at §38: 'The anima is most minutely sentient of every change occurring in the entire body...but...we are not conscious of any other changes than such as specifically affect the cortex of the cerebrum'. Since 'sentient' is a synonym for 'consciousness' this might explicitly state that there is more than one conscious field in the same body.

Swedenborg appears to regard pure intellect as yet another conscious field distinct from our familiar one[44] but below the internal.[45] I would conjecture that it is the same as the interior man as described in *Arcana Caelestia*—and similar to the higher rational levels of Islamic thought. At §126 of *Rational Psychology* he states 'on the pure intellect depends sensation, no sensation, or perception of sensation being possible unless the nature of what is received is understood by an interior or superior power'. This is not, however, the pure intellect of Descartes. For Descartes in *The Principles*,[46] says the pure intellect is that which apprehends a chiliagon (i.e. in modern terminology imageless thought), or thought for which such images as may accompany it do not adequately represent the content.[47]

In other words Swedenborg identifies at least three conscious fields: internal or soul; interior or pure intellect; and everyday consciousness consisting of reason (the human intellect), imagination and sense.

The Self

So far, I have described the older ideas of the soul[48] or mind negatively as something distinct from the physical (except for the concept of 'consciousness' which seems a late philosophical idea). It is worth asking if there is any attribute of the soul which might be defined positively, that is pre-philosophical and as old as the notion of soul itself. And there is. It is the self. But this notion is perhaps even more difficult to define than soul or mind.

Common words for self are 'I' and all other first person pronouns. 'Person' at times, is also used as an English synonym for it. My *Oxford Latin Dictionary* (apart from *se* and *ego*) gives *proprium* as 'one's own' and also 'property in the sense of characteristic'. *Proprium* has been interpreted as selfhood in some translations of Swedenborg.[49] The *Oxford Latin Dictionary* also gives 'person' as 'homo' which throws light on such of Swedenborg's sayings as that the spirit is the interior man[50] and that the interior man lives as man after death. *Al nafs* in Arabic has connotations both of the soul, pride and selfishness.

That the self is linked to the soul in mythology appears from the *Odyssey*.[51] The souls from the underworld appear to Odysseus and lament their wretched life in fields of asphodel (a plant used to adorn graves) which is not to be compared with the life in this world. Many peoples have had similar ideas of ghosts but my point is that there is no doubt that the ghosts are the same people they were in life (i.e. the 'selves' are the same). However, it is unclear as to what this self is. The self, familiar as it seems, gives rise to paradoxes, as Locke and Hume in particular realised.[52] The problems concern its endurance and its value. It is an object in the (brief) conscious field yet it endures through a lifetime of successive fields. It is responsible, it 'owns' its actions, which involves endurance and value (merit). Ethically it is thought to have a unique value ('end in itself'), yet it is not clear what its features are at all let alone how they can be valued. Pride is also relevant here.[53] If we turn to the theological definition of person we find 'intellectual substance', which is clear but not helpful. For intellectual we may substitute consciousness, and consciousness surely must be linked to the self. But substance does not help because as Locke may have been the first to point out, the endurance of the self and of a substance are not the same. The lack of philosophic interest in Swedenborg by philosophers must be partly due to the fact that most of the problems of Western philosophy do not overlap with Swedenborg's problems. But with the self they do.

Question: Is the self the conscious field?

Answer: No, because the conscious field has almost no temporal depth, the specious present being of the order of a second(s). I have indeed heard a Japanese person say that he was not worried about health risks from smoking because he did not care about when he was old. So it is possible that some people are unable to recognise self-identity over a long time. But everyone makes provision for hours ahead—far longer than the duration of the conscious field.

Q: Is the self the soul?

A: According to the Platonic dialogue *Alcibiades,* cited in William Hamilton's *Lectures on Metaphysics,* we *are* a soul rather than we *have* a soul. This however, seems somewhat broad (rather, it would seem that the self is a specific part or aspect of the soul). It would certainly seem that there can only be one self per soul (and one self per conscious field). The apparent splitting of consciousness in hypnosis and multiple personality is however puzzling (see below).[54]

Q: Is the self the internal man?

A: The Indian term *atman* seems to be the same as Swedenborg's internal man and is translated as self. But this is above consciousness and separate from the decisions of the will in Indian thought and in Swedenborg at *Arcana Caelestia* §1999. So its status in relation to the self is baffling.

Q: Locke's doctrine[55] is that the self is a series of conscious fields tied together by memory. This seems to explain why a person is unique, and perhaps some form of association of ideas would explain why we provide for future conscious fields. Of course it implies that someone with irrevocable amnesia is no longer the same person. But is that unreasonable?

A: It doesn't explain the value of the individual. Nor can I see that it explains the transmission of responsibility from one conscious field to another (i.e. the *karma* chain of the Buddhists).

Q: What about equating the self and the will?

A: Leaving aside, for the moment, the difficult account he gives of *proprium*, Swedenborg at times describes the will is the soul itself[56] by which it might be presumed he means self. This seems more promising to me than identifying self with consciousness. But there are still a couple of things this seems not to include: 1) the unique value of the person or self; and 2) the nature of responsibility for good and evil choices. Let me take them one by one.

1. Why should a particular will have a unique value when every member of a species—even the human—pursues similar ends, apart from the choice between good and evil? Isn't this like attributing enormous value to every point on the personality scales derived from tests?[57] However difficult it is to conceive the importance of the difference, Swedenborg does say in his *The True Christian Religion,* at §417, that it is on account of the ends they pursue that people are valued not for their persons. This seems to contradict Kant's view that an individual is an end in himself, which is surely the essence of love. However I think Swedenborg's statement need not be as harsh as it sounds. We have to suppose that when Swedenborg says the neighbour is not the person at §417 of *The True Christian Religion*, he is using person in a special sense, (cf *James* 2:1). If we take it that in some sense an individual is their own unique end, then valuing them for themselves and for their end or use are the same.[58]

2. As for responsibility it is tempting to replace Locke's concept of the memory linking conscious fields with the interior memory.[59] For Swedenborg himself says this is the book of a man's life out of which he is judged. However some caution is in order. Swedenborg

says that the things in it are *chiefly* those of the will. (If there are other contents it means the interior memory concept does not isolate the factor of responsibility from others).

There are two other aspects of equal importance of Swedenborg's doctrine of the self which I can't elaborate here. One is that Swedenborg speaks of self love as pride.[60] The second is in relation to the self and free will he says that all things good and evil flow into man from outside[61] a highly paradoxical position. In some sense Swedenborg here dissolves wholly or partly one of the self's functions ownership of good and evil acts.

Multiple Souls

In ancient times people sometimes addressed their souls, which can be seen in *Judges* 5:21 and the Egyptian dialogue of a man with his *ba*.[62] Hercules, after death has two souls, one with the gods, the other in the underworld.[63] To conclude, I would briefly like to address the subject of multiple souls and why nearly all theories of the soul involve the notion of multiple souls in the same body (which runs counter to common sense as well as to Cartesian philosophy). In some of the following instances, maybe all, the view is that there are different *conscious fields* or *wills* in the same body. How can this be? Which soul is, or contains, me? Or at least which is to control the voice and limbs? Descartes generally agrees with common sense, the only bizarre point in his theories being that animals do not have souls. No doubt this contributed to the hideous vivisection practised subsequently.[64] The other theories mentioned in the following appear somewhat more difficult to common sense. However, in modern pyschology there are well attested cases of phenomena involving the splitting of consciousness. There are cases in hypnosis, of 'dissociation', where something like this can happen: for example, an individual under hypnosis is asked to put his left hand in ice water. When asked if this hurt replies 'no'. In the meantime his right hand, unbeknown to the subject, is writing 'It hurts like hell'.[65] Then there are also cases of multiple personality (e.g. Morton Prince)[66] where one of the personalities of an individual was co-conscious with another who did not know of her. These, while not involving degrees may make the following theories, some of which involve degrees, more plausible. I will review them historically.

According to E B Tylor, the Karens, a people of Burma, distinguish between the *la*, 'the personal life phantom', and *thah* 'the responsible moral soul'. The Dakota Indians say man has four souls: one stays with the corpse, one in the village, one going in the air and one to the land of the spirits.[67]

Again, in Indian culture,[68] we find a twofold distinction in the notion of *atman* which signifies an immediate union with God detached from the fate of the lower soul. The case is similar with an account of a Chinese view given in A Cottrell's *Oxford Dictionary of Mythology*.[69] Here two souls are ascribed to men, the *hun* and the *pho*. On death the *hun* goes to heaven, the *pho* to a hell of torment (the Yellow Springs, a place beneath the earth). This eventuality is ascribed to everybody. However there are varying accounts of the fate of some souls, presumably the *pho*, going to heaven. I have also seen Chinese money burnt for use of one's dead relatives in hell and am told the money for those in heaven is in less demand because few are thought to go there. So it would seem that one view is there is a heaven for some *phos* as well as for all *huns*. What is perhaps surprising is that Swedenborg gives a similar account in *Arcana Caelestia* §1999 where there is a heaven of human internals without which man would be mortal, and all (whether in heaven or hell) have their internals there.

Plato in the *Republic* and *Timaeus* has no less than *two* lower souls—one prone to lust or greed, the other to anger—as well as one higher, the rational. He considers the angry soul to be more noble, while the lustful (or greedy) soul is the mediator of divination and art.

Aristotle offers a threefold division of the soul into rational, animal and vegetable.[70] A distinguishing feature of Aristotle's account of the vegetable soul is that it plays a part in nutrition. Nevertheless, the vital agency credited by Aristotle as the lowest soul in his hierarchy, is the highest agency for Swedenborg in his *Word Explained* §150. Nowadays the intervention of any non-physical factor—vital force—in physiology would be anathema to most scientists, understandably in view of the success of biochemical explanations of life. However, Eysenck and Sargent record several apparently paranormal psychokinetic effects on plant growth and on the activity of trypsin in vitro.[71]

The next landmark figure is Paul. In describing the combats between the spirit and the flesh, we find *esa* translates as 'inner man' (interior) (*Romans* 7:22), and *nous* (*mens*) as 'mind' (*Romans* 7:23). At *Romans* 8:7 we find *phronema tes sarkos* for 'mind of the flesh'. In *1 Corinthians* 2:14 *phusikos anthropos* stands for natural man and in

1 Corinthians 2:15, *pneumaticos* means the spiritual [man]. In *1 Thessalonians* 5:23 we have in one verse, spirit (*pneuma*), soul (*psyche*) and body (*soma*) (in the *Vulgate*, *spiritus*, *anima* and *corpus*).

The communion of saints in the Apostle's Creed is like Swedenborg's concept of influx from the world or spirits, implying that more than one soul can affect the same body.

Apollinaris the younger, (b. 310 AD, Bishop of Laodicea) in order to combat the Arians, worked out an interpretation of Aristotle's scheme to explain the divine nature of Jesus Christ. His writings, condemned to be destroyed by the church survived by being disguised as productions of such orthodox writers as Athanasius and Gregory of Nyssa. According to Apollinaris, God was present in Jesus carrying out the functions of the rational soul and Jesus therefore lacked any human rational soul of his own. Swedenborg in contrast, again at *Arcana Caelestia* §1999, suggests that Jesus lacked not a rational degree, but an internal, the Father acting immediately on his rational. Therefore it can be seen that the degrees of the soul are of the highest theological importance and might be expected to be a matter of revelation. And indeed, because the internal is above consciousness, one might expect it could only be known by revelation. But in that case it is hard to account for Swedenborg's knowledge of the internal in *Rational Psychology* §137.

Islamic thought [72] remains with Aristotle in regarding the rational as highest, however, it subdivides it into many levels some of which are above consciousness. Thus this would seem to answer to Swedenborg's pure intellect discussed above (the interior rather than the internal). Muslim thinkers conceived of ten levels of understanding (heavens) proceeding successively from God and all above human consciousness, which can be compared to Swedenborg's six degrees of Truth Divine at *Arcana Caelestia* §8443. According to the Persian philosopher Avicenna (980-1037) each level is associated with an archangel, the lowest of which makes contact with the highest level of human understanding. The lowest of these super intelligent beings is sometimes identified with Gabriel who is believed to have mediated the dictation of the *Koran* to Mohammed. These archangels are like shared souls and some concluded that there was no immortality at the human level which is below theirs. In a development of Aristotle's views Avicenna also subdivides each of Aristotle's souls into four levels, of which the highest resembles the lowest of the next soul above it. Thus the highest animal resembles the lowest rational.

Accordingly, Mulla Sadra argues that the levels of the soul below the understanding have subtle matter associated with them. Sohravardi (unknown-1191) speaks of a lordly light within the soul representing God, the light of lights, which may correspond to Swedenborg's notion of the internal. It is also possible however that Sohravardi might have accepted Avicenna's psychology in which case the lordly light would be the rational. Sohravardi may have been influenced by Zoroastrianism. In any case he was considered a sufficient maverick to be put to death by the chivalrous Saladin. Sohravardi also recognised an intermediate plane the *mundus imaginalis*[73] which was not in space and time in the same way as the material world.[74] Swedenborg's contemporary Shah Wali Allah (1703-1762) also spoke of this world of images as containing archetypes on which religious rituals are founded. Thus he held something similar to Swedenborg's concept of correspondences.

Finally, returning to the west, G W Leibniz (1646-1716), Swedenborg's older contemporary, (and perhaps the anonymous philosopher of deep insight mentioned at *Arcana Caelestia* §6326), propoese that the bodies of men and animals (and even inanimate bodies) contain and consist of innumerable souls (*monads*). This is not a difference of degree in itself, but in each human body there is a rational *monad*, which is hence a degree above the other animal *monads*. All souls, both rational and animal, survive death until eternity and also pre-exist before birth. Sensations are the subjective appearance of psychological processes in other minds both now and after death.

Most recently psychoanalysis has developed the concept of the unconscious influenced by the above mentioned phenomena of hypnosis and multiple personality. The unconscious, is distinct from the 'I', but probably a second conscious field distinct from normal consciousness and hence might therefore be considered another soul(s). The earliest philosopher of the unconscious was perhaps Leibniz, followed by Maine de Biran (1766-1824), J F Herbart (1776-1841), William Hamilton (1788-1854) and Eduard von Hartmann (1842-1906). Sigmund Freud (1856-1939) of course thought of it as inferior in goodness and intelligence to everyday ego-consciousness, as did his predecessor E Hartmann. But C G Jung (1875-1961), and the eminent psychic researcher F W H Myers,[75] conceived of higher tendencies there. At worst the unconscious answers to Swedenborg's concept of hell but is more usually equivalent to his concept of the world of spirits, especially as Freud, Jung and Myers all conceived of the unconscious as permeable to telepathic influences. We can see that these theories too fall under the heading of multiple souls—for multiple conscious fields are related to multiple non-physical factors in one body—though it is quite conceivable that there are also non-physical factors which are not conscious (e.g. the sense data).

Notes

[1] One definition of Swedenborg's theory of degrees can be found in Michael Stanley's essay *Ladder of Ascent,* published by the Swedenborg Society, 1976.

[2] *Timaeus, Republic* and *The Sophist.* Plato. Loeb, 1929.

[3] *On the Soul [De Anima].* Aristotle. Peripatetic, 1981.

[4] *Study of Instinct.* N Tinbergen. OUP Clarendon, 1989. *Act of Creation.* A Koestler. Macmillan, 1964.

[5] *Arcana Caelestia.* E Swedenborg. §1999. Translated by J Elliott. The Swedenborg Society, 1983-99. See also *Rational Psychology* §38 and §127.

[6] *English Works.* Thomas Hobbes. Berlin, 1839. *Essui Sur l'origine des Connaissances Humaines.* E Condillac. Galilee, 1973. (See also his, *Traite des Sensations*). *A Treatise on Human Nature.* David Hume. Penguin, 1985. First English edition 1739. The English Associationist School might be listed as Thomas Hobbes (1588-1674), J Locke (1672-1704), Revd J Gay (1694-1745), D Hartley (1705-1757), J Priestly (1733-1804)—discoverer of oxygen and controversialist regarding 'Baron Swedenborg' with Hindmarsh, James Mill (1773-1836). See also T Brown, note 31.

[7] *Psychology of Learning.* Hulse, Deese, Egeth. Fifth edition McGraw. Hill, 1980.

[8] *Molecular Biology of the Cell.* Alberts et al. Garland, 1994. *Computability and Logic.* G Boolos and R C Jeffry. Cambridge, 1980. See also C D Broad's *The Mind and its place in Nature.* RKP, 1925.

[9] *Rational Psychology.* E Swedenborg. §38. Swedenborg Scientific Association. USA. 2001.

[10] *Early Greek Philosophy.* Penguin, 1987. *Oxford Companion to Philosophy.* Ed. T Honderich. OUP, 1995.

[11] *English Works.* Thomas Hobbes. Berlin, 1839.

[12] *Scientific Thought.* C D Broad. Humanities, 1969. See also, *The View from Nowhere.* Thomas Nagel. Oxford, 1986.

[13] *Essay on Human Understanding.* J Locke. Penguin, 1987.

[14] *Human Knowledge: Its Scope and Limits.* Bertrand Russell. Allen Unwin, 1948.

[15] *Scientific Thought.* C D Broad. Humanities, 1969.

[16] *Enquiry into the Human Mind*. Thomas Reid. See *Reid's Works*.

[17] For a fuller account of relativity and sense data see: C D Broad's *Scientific Thought*. For a fuller account of quantum physics see d'Abro's, *The Rise of the New Physics*. Dover, 1951.

[18] At *Arcana Caelestia* §444-46, Swedenborg appears to say the spirit is extended seemingly contradicting *Arcana Caelestia* §1273 where he says there is only apparent space in the other life.

[19] *Dialogues of Hylas and Philonous*. George Berkeley. *Works*, Edited by A A Luce and T E Jessop. Nine vols. London, 1947-59. (Was the immaterialist Berkeley one of these Bishops who received copies of short works from Swedenborg in the late 1750's and who 'so shamefully rejected them' as mentioned in *The Spiritual Diary* §6101.2? Or did his status as a church of Ireland bishop mean that he did not get sent them — an intriguing question for historians).

[20] See Maria Crasta'a essay elsewhere in this volume.

[21] *Rational Psychology* §126. *Ontology*. E Swedenborg. §34. Swedenborg Scientific Association, 1901.

[22] *Rational Psychology* §494.

[23] *Rational Psychology* §498—§503.

[24] *Arcana Caelestia* §1999.

[25] *Rational Psychology* §490.

[26] *Arcana Caelestia* §322, §1630.

[27] *Arcana Caelestia* §1274.

[28] *African Religions and Philosophy*. J Mbiti. Heinemann, 1969.

[29] From a different perspective see C D Broad's *Lectures on Psychical Research*. RKP, 1962.

[30] It is at least possible to argue that life after death is conceivable from a materialist stand point. Those who have done so include the astronomer V A Firsoff in our own time and M Gosala as far back as 600 BC (who in the Jain tradition, is in relation to Mahavira as Judas Iscariot is to Christ in the *Gospels*). Swedenborg himself, of course, in his early work seems to have fallen into this category of materialists who believed in survival after death as already stated. See note 21.

[31] See T Brown's *Lectures on the Philosophy of the Human Mind*. Longmans, 1951. First English edition 1850.

[32] *Rational Psychology* §488 and §494. See also T Brown's *Lectures on the Philosophy of the Human Mind*.

[33] *Works*. Edited by A A Luce and T E Jessop. 9 vols. London, 1947-59.

[34] *Buddhists Scriptures*. Edward Conze. Penguin, 1959.

[35] *Religion, Philosophy & Psychical Research*. C D Broad. RKP, 1953.

[36] ibid.

[37] See William James' *Principles of Psychology*. Dover, 1957.

[38] *Sleep*. I Oswald. Penguin. Four editions published between 1966-1980.

[39] *Essay on Human Understanding.* J Locke. Penguin, 1987.
[40] See the Index to *Arcana Caelestia* reference in article 'perception' to §7680.
[41] *Arcana Caelestia* §3528.
[42] See Oswald's, *Sleep*.
[43] Compare with Epicharmus of the 5th Century BC who stated 'What sees is mind, what hears is mind, the ear and eye are deaf and blind'. Cited by William Hamilton in *Notes to Dissertation on* [Thomas] *Reid*.
[44] *Rational Psychology* §131 and §136.
[45] *Rational Psychology* §127 and §137.
[46] *Principles of Philosophy*. R Descartes. Philosophical Works. Cambridge, 1911.
[47] See *The Penguin Dictionary of Psychology*. Article 'imageless thought'.
[48] Whenever I use the term soul on my own account rather than quoting Swedenborg I have used it to mean the entire mind or 'psi-factor' rather than in the special sense Swedenborg uses in *Rational Psychology*, as just discussed.
[49] *Arcana Caelestia* §8, §214; *Rational Psychology* §301.
[50] *Arcana Caelestia* §6054; *Rational Psychology* §344.
[51] *Odyssey,* Book XI 660 and Book XXIV, line 14-15. Everyman, 1992. Translated by William Cowper.
[52] Since Swedenborg, Hume and Buddhists all have views of illusions appertaining to the self how do they overlap? Hume denies even a momentary self. Buddhists, according to Edward Conze in his *Buddhist Scripture* (Penguin, 1955) deny a permanent self (at least):
    'Our whole life and personality
    is bound up in a single moment
    and rapidly that moment passes'.
Swedenborg denies the ownership of good and evil actions at *Arcana Caelestia* §6324 and §6325.
[53] See David Hume's *A Treatise of Human Nature*; Book 2 *Of the Passions*.
[54] See Melzack, R. *Challenge of Pain*. Penguin, 1988. Morton Prince. *Dissociation of a Personality,* Longmans, 1905. William James. *Principles of Psychology*. Dover, 1957.
[55] *Essay on Human Understanding.* Locke, J. Penguin, 1987.
[56] *Arcana Caelestia* §10076.
[57] See *Individual Differences*. M Eysenck. Lawrence Erlbaum, 1994. *Sense and Nonsense in Psychology*. H J Eysenck. Penguin. 1956.
[58] *Divine Providence*. E Swedenborg. cf. §309.and §57. The Swedenborg Society, 1988.
[59] *Arcana Caelestia* §2474, §9386.
[60] *Arcana Caelestia* §8678, §8995. *Rational Psychology* §27-28. On this point see also Hume's *Of the Passions* Book 2.
[61] *Arcana Caelestia* §848 and §6324-5; *Divine Providence*. §58.

[62] See *The Ancient Egyptian and his Literature* by Wallis-Budge.
[63] *Odyssey*. Book XI, 935. Same translation as note 51.
[64] *The Cerebrum*. E Swedenborg. §127. The Swedenborg Scientific Association, 1938.
[65] *Challenge of Pain*. R Melzack and P Wall. Penguin, 1988.
[66] *Dissociation of a Personality*. Morton Prince. Longmans, 1905.
[67] *From Primitives to Zen*. M Eliade. Chicago, 1966.
[68] See *History of Indian Philosophy*. Dasgupta. Banarsidji, 1996.
[69] *Oxford Dictionary of Mythology*. A Cottrell. Oxford University Press, 1986.
[70] *On the Soul*. Aristotle.
[71] *Explaining the Unexplained*. H J Eysench and C Sargent. Weidenfield and Nicolson, 1982. *The Word Explained*. E Swedenborg. Academy of the New Church, 1928.
[72] *Great Thinkers of the Eastern World*. I P McCreal. Harper Collins, 1995.
[73] For Swedenborg the *Mundus Imaginalis* can be seen as equivalent to the level of imagination, spoken of as 'internal sight' in *Rational Psychology* cf §72.
[74] See *Arcana Caelestia* cf §1274.
[75] *Human Personality and its Survival of Bodily Death*. F W H Myers. 1903.

Schopenhauer as Reader of Swedenborg

Gregory R Johnson

Arthur Schopenhauer (1788-1860) is widely known as the first Western philosopher of note to delve seriously into the esoteric philosophies of the East, Hinduism and Buddhism in particular.[1] Although the outlines of Schopenhauer's philosophy were in place before his discovery of Eastern thought, this encounter affected the subsequent development of his philosophy in many ways.[2] Less widely known is Schopenhauer's equally broad reading in the Western esoteric tradition, including the writings of Emanuel Swedenborg. Schopenhauer's library included works by Meister Eckhart, Ramon Lull, Angelus Silesius, Nicholas of Cusa, Marsilio Ficino, Giovanni Pico della Mirandola, Henricus Cornelius Agrippa, Paracelsus, Giordano Bruno, Tomasso Campanella, Jakob Boehme, Jane Leade, John Pordage, Johannes Tauler, Johann Heinrich Jung-Stilling, Franz von Baader, and Karl von Eckarthausen, as well as Swedenborg.[3] It also included a large collection of books on animal magnetism, clairvoyance, and spirit apparitions, including the multi-volume *Archiv für den Thierischen Magnetismus* [*Archive of Animal Magnetism*].[4] Many of these works are extensively annotated in Schopenhauer's hand. The list of the books on paranormal phenomena alone occupies thirty-two pages in the catalogue of Schopenhauer's library and its marginalia published by Arthur Hübscher.[5]

In this essay, I shall focus on Schopenhauer's encounter with Swedenborg. I shall argue two points. First, Schopenhauer took Swedenborg's writings and the claim that he was a clairvoyant seriously, meaning that he looked to Swedenborg as a potential source of important truths. Second, although Schopenhauer and Swedenborg share the same basic metaphysical outlook according to which such phenomena as clairvoyance are possible, Schopenhauer's metaphysical commitment to the idea that the individual soul perishes at death is deeply incompatible with Swedenborg's visionary experiences. Thus, although Schopenhauer adamantly defends the possibility of clairvoyance, the incompatibility of Swedenborg's visions with his own outlook leads Schopenhauer in the end to reject the truth of Swedenborg's visions and to try to explain them away.

1. Schopenhauer's Familiarity with Swedenborg's Writings

Upon his death, Schopenhauer's library contained two volumes of Swedenborg. First is the *Prodromus Philosophiae ratiocinantis de Infinito, et causa finali creationis, deque mechanismo operationis animae et corporis* [*Forerunner of a Reasoned Philosophy Concerning the Infinite and the Final Cause of Creation, also The Mechanism of the Operation of the Soul and the Body*].[6] Published in 1734, this work predates Swedenborg's first visions of the spiritual world. Schopenhauer's copy is now lost, so there is no way to determine whether he annotated it or what he had to say. The other Swedenborg volume is a 1782 French translation comprising *Heaven and Hell* and *Earths in the Universe: Les merveilles du ciel et de l'enfer et des terres planétaires et astrals. D'après le témoignage de ses yeux et de ses oreilles* [*The Marvels of Heaven and Hell and the Planets in our Solar System and in the Stars. According to the Testimony of the Eyes and Ears*].[7] This volume contains an interesting note in Schopenhauer's hand that we shall examine below.

There is reason to believe that Schopenhauer also read Swedenborg's 1769 *Opusculum, De Commercio Animae et Corporis* [*The Interaction of Soul and Body*],[8] for Schopenhauer mentions Swedenborg's encounter with Aristotle and Christian Wolff in the spiritual world, which is described in §19 of that work.[9] There is, furthermore, evidence that Schopenhauer read Swedenborg's major 1771 work *Vera Christiana Religio* [*The True Christian Religion*],[10] for he paraphrases and comments upon a passage in an unpublished manuscript that we will examine in the next section.[11]

Another source of Schopenhauer's knowledge of Swedenborg is Kant's 1766 book *Träume eines Geistershehers* [*Dreams of a Spirit-Seer*].[12] Although it is rife with snide and dismissive comments about Swedenborg, this volume, along with Kant's 1763 letter to Charlotte von Knobloch, is history's primary source of information on three of Swedenborg's most famous clairvoyant feats, which are known as the affairs of the Queen's Secret, the Stockholm Fire, and the Lost Receipt.[13] Schopenhauer's copy of *Dreams* shows evidence of careful study, particularly of part II, chapter 2, 'Ecstatic Journey of an Enthusiast Through the Spirit World', in which Kant presents his digest of Swedenborg's accounts of the spiritual world in the *Arcana Coelestia*. In the margins of Kant's exposition, Schopenhauer provides citations to the appropriate passages of the French edition of *Heaven and Hell*.[14] Schopenhauer also had access to Kant's Letter to Charlotte von Knobloch, which was first published as an appendix to Ludwig Ernst Borowski's biography of Kant, *Darstellung des Lebens und Charakters Immanuel Kants*.[15] In November 1814, Schopenhauer checked out a copy from the Dresden Public Library for a month, then later acquired his own copy.[16]

2. Swedenborg and Schopenhauer's Philosophical Style

Schopenhauer was primarily interested in Swedenborg as a clairvoyant and spirit-seer. Before turning to this topic, however, I wish to examine Schopenhauer's earliest recorded remark on Swedenborg, from a manuscript dated 1817:

In the *Vera christiana religio* [*The True Christian Religion*] §400 Swedenborg says that, 'The egoistical man with his bodily eyes certainly sees the rest as men, but with his spiritual eyes he sees as men only himself and his relations, whilst the rest he sees only as masks'. According to their innermost meaning, these words are the same as Kant's precept that, 'We should never consider others merely as means but as ends in themselves'. But how differently expressed is the idea; how vivid, sharp and to the point, graphic and immediately adequate are the words of Swedenborg (whose manner and way of thinking I do not usually find enjoyable), and how indirect, abstract and expressed through a derived connotation are the words of Kant![17]

First, it should be noted that the first set of words in quotation marks are not Swedenborg's words, but Schopenhauer's paraphrase of the gist of the first paragraph of *The True Christian Religion* §400. Second, Schopenhauer's remark that he 'usually' does not enjoy Swedenborg's 'manner and way of thinking' implies a wider acquaintance with Swedenborg's works. Furthermore, although Swedenborg's writings do contain some striking images, they are mostly rather dry, so Schopenhauer really cannot be faulted for finding Swedenborg's style to be most of the time uncongenial. (As Henry James Sr. was wont to observe, however, Swedenborg's lack of stylistic savour actually supports his veracity.[18] He is not trying too hard to persuade, which in itself is persuasive.) Third, Schopenhauer is stylistically the greatest German writer of philosophy, and one of the greatest philosophical stylists of all time. Thus for Schopenhauer to praise Swedenborg's style, albeit it in a limited and qualified manner, is still high praise indeed.

The sincerest flattery, however, is the recurrence of this Swedenborgian trope more than twenty years later in §22 of Schopenhauer's 1839 treatise *On the Basis of Morality*:

> Thus there is the man to whom all others are invariably non-ego, and who in fact ultimately regards only his own person as truly real, looking upon others virtually only as phantoms, attributing to them only a relative existence insofar as they may be a means or an obstacle to his ends. Thus there remains an immeasurable difference, a deep gulf, between his person and all that is non-ego. He exists exclusively in his own person, and sees all reality and the whole world perish with his own self in death.[19]

A more distant echo appears in §165 of Schopenhauer's essay, 'Additional Remarks on the Doctrine of the Affirmation of the Will-to-Live', first published in 1851 in volume two of *Parerga and Paraliomena*, Schopenhauer's essays:

> A noble character will not readily complain about his own fate; on the contrary, what Hamlet says in praise of Horatio will apply to him:
>
> > for thou hast been
> > As one, in suffering all, that suffers nothing.

This can be understood from the fact that such a man, recognising his own true nature in others and thus sharing their fate, almost invariably sees around him an even harder lot than his own and so cannot bring himself to complain of the latter. An ignoble egoist, on the other hand, who limits all reality to himself and regards others as mere masks and phantoms, will take no part in their fate, but will devote the whole of his sympathy and interest to his own; the results of this will then be great sensitiveness and frequent complaints.[20]

These stylistic echoes of Swedenborg are by no means the only ones in Schopenhauer's writings.[21] They are a far cry from signs of philosophical influence, but they do indicate that Schopenhauer read Swedenborg's works with care and sensitivity.

3. Schopenhauer's Theory of Spirit-Seeing

The main reason Schopenhauer read Swedenborg was a deep and abiding fascination with paranormal phenomena, evinced by his library, his manuscript remains and his published writings. Schopenhauer published two accounts of paranormal phenomena. First is his chapter on 'Animal Magnetism and Magic' in his 1836 book *On the Will in Nature*.[22] Second is his extensive 1851 'Essay on Spirit-Seeing and Related Phenomena'.[23] This essay, which occupies ninety-eight pages in the Suhrkamp edition of Schopenhauer's *Collected Works* and eighty-three pages in Payne's English translation, is more than fifty per cent longer than Kant's entire book *Dreams of a Spirit-Seer* and is based on vastly more research. It also stands out as Schopenhauer's worst-written work. Rambling, prolix, disorganised and often dull, it is in need of sections and sub-sections for easier reading and comprehension. The subject matter demands a formal treatise, not a breezy and sometimes annoyingly digressive essay.

In the 'Essay' Schopenhauer attempts to offer a single theory that explains a number of different paranormal phenomena: (1) *animal-magnetism*, now known as hypnosis, in which the hypnotist places the patient in a trance-like state which allows the hypnotist to exert his will over the patient and the patient to access levels of consciousness that are unavailable to normal waking consciousness, (2) *somnambulism*, which is not confined merely to sleep-walking, but includes any activity engaged in while unconscious or in a trance, including under hypnosis, (3) *clairvoyance*, which means sensing things that cannot be physically sensed because of great distances of time or space or a difference of metaphysical status, e.g., dead people, (4) *magic*, which means action at a distance analogous to sensing at a distance, (5) *prophecy* of the future, (6) *apparitions* of the living and the dead, and (7) *mediumship*, meaning communication with the spirits of the dead.

Schopenhauer's neo-Kantian metaphysics offers the foundation for his explanation of these phenomena. First, Schopenhauer holds to the Kantian distinction between phenomena and the thing-in-itself. These are different because the finite, determinate nature of our cognitive faculties implies that we can experience things not as they are in themselves, but only insofar as they can be given to us. Second, again following Kant, Schopenhauer argues that we experience things as spatio-temporal objects subject to causal laws because it is the nature of our mind to do so. Space, time and causality constitute the structure of the phenomenal realm, not necessarily of reality in itself. While Kant was himself mostly agnostic on the nature of ultimate reality and would claim only that we cannot know if the thing-in-itself is also spatio-temporal and subject to causal laws, Schopenhauer positively affirms that the thing-in-itself lies outside of space and time and is not subject to causal laws. Third, again taking his lead from Kant but pushing beyond him, Schopenhauer affirms that the thing-in-itself is will. Furthermore, Schopenhauer argues that since the will lies outside of space and time, which are the principles of individuation, the will is undifferentiated. Insofar as each phenomenal individual has his roots in the thing-in-itself, we are all, in ourselves, one. Fourth, human consciousness has a number of levels. The highest level of consciousness is wakeful, worldly, self-conscious awareness, which is also the most individuated level of consciousness. As we descend through the gradations of consciousness, we become less self-conscious and less individuated. When we descend below the threshold of self-consciousness to the unconscious or subconscious mind, we leave individuation further behind and approach the undifferentiated will, which lies outside of space, time and the causal order.

An additional element of Schopenhauer's account is his notion of the 'dream-organ'.[24] In dreams, we experience things that are not given to our external senses. Our experiences are, therefore, generated from within, by means of the dream-organ. The dream-organ explains not only dreams, but also spirit apparitions. Spirits do not appear by stimulating our senses, but by stimulating the dream-organ while we are awake. Because we are awake when the dream-organ is stimulated, we automatically transpose the dream image into the outer realm. Yet other people cannot see these apparitions because these apparitions do not—and indeed cannot—stimulate their external senses, but only the dream-organs of those who are susceptible to apparitions. Schopenhauer's notion of the dream-organ is also derived from Kant, from *Dreams of a Spirit-Seer*.[25]

Magic, clairvoyant cognition of 'the hidden, the absent, the remote and even that which still slumbers in the womb of the future', and other paranormal phenomena seem to suspend space, time and the causal order.[26] This is not, however, incomprehensible given Schopenhauer's metaphysics, for space, time and causality are merely how the world appears to our ordinary consciousness. They are part of the world as representation. But if we leave ordinary consciousness behind, we will enter a new world where space, time, and causality are annulled. We will enter the world of the will. Schopenhauer's theory is that the paranormal phenomena listed above involve trance-like states, whether self-induced, spontaneous, or induced by another. In these trance-states, we descend down the scale of consciousness and approach the realm of the undifferentiated will, where the distinctions between near and far, and between past, present and future have no meaning. In Schopenhauer's words:

> Animal magnetism, sympathetic cures, magic, second sight, dreaming the real, spirit seeing and visions of all kinds are kindred phenomena, branches of one stem. They afford certain and irrefutable proof of a nexus of entities that rests on an order of things entirely different from nature. For her foundation nature has the laws of space, time and causality, whereas that other order is more deep-seated, original and immediate. Therefore the first and most universal (because purely formal) laws of nature are not applicable to it. Accordingly, time and space no longer separate individuals and their separation and isolation, which are due to those very forms, no longer place insuperable barriers in the way of the communication of thoughts and the direct influence of the will. Thus changes are brought about in a way quite different

from that of physical causality with the continuous chain of its links; in other words, they are produced merely by virtue of an act of will that is brought to light in a special manner and thereby intensified to a higher potential beyond the individual. Accordingly, the peculiar characteristic of all the animal phenomena here considered is *visio in distans et actio in distans* [seeing at a distance and acting at a distance], both as regards time and space.[27]

Animal magnetism is explained by the fact that the common root of all is the will. The hypnotist, by inducing a trance-like state in his patient, puts the individual will out of commission and opens the patient up to the influxes of the universal will, through the medium of which the hypnotist exercises his will over the patient. *Somnambulism* is ultimately explained by the scale of consciousness and the relative superficiality of the self-conscious mind when compared to the vastness of the subconscious or unconscious. We know more than we know we know. We can do more than we know we can do. *Clairvoyance* is possible if we can sense things through the medium of the will, where distances of space and time do not exist. Since the normal senses are not used in clairvoyant cognition, such experiences enter consciousness through the dream-organ. *Magic* is possible if we can act on things through the medium of the will, where not only space and time, but also the laws of causality do not exist. *Prophecy* is possible if we can access the realm of the will, which is 'that mechanism which is hidden in the background and from which everything originates...so that which is seen externally, that is, through our optical lens of time, as merely something that will come in the future, is already at this moment present in that mechanism'.[28] Prophetic visions enter consciousness through the dream-organ. *Apparitions* of the living and the dead are caused by the will of the persons who appear. Their wills cause images of themselves to be communicated through the medium of the will and to appear in the dream-organs of parties who are susceptible to such apparitions. Finally, according to Schopenhauer's theory, *mediumship*, meaning actual communication with the spirits of the dead, is not possible.

Schopenhauer stresses again and again that apparitions of the dead are caused by dead persons *while they are still alive*, and their effects linger long after they are dead, like the light of burnt-out stars. He claims that an image of a person is affixed to particular places and things by their intense emotions, and these images can enter the consciousness of sensitive people through their dream-organs. Schopenhauer's examples of apparitions are the stuff of Romantic literature and opera: murder victims dressed as they were when they were killed, misers guarding their treasure hordes, dead lovers haunting their living beloveds, etc. In Schopenhauer's words:

> From what has been said, it is obvious that the immediate reality of an actually existing object is not to be imputed to a ghost that appears in this way, although indirectly a reality does underlie it. Thus what we see there is certainly not the deceased man himself, but a mere *eidolon*, a picture of him who once existed which originates in the dream-organ of a man attuned to it and is brought about by some remnant relic, some trace that was left behind... Accordingly, a spirit apparition of the kind we are here considering certainly does stand in objective relation to the *former* state of the person who appears, but certainly not to his *present* state, for it does not take any active part therein, and so from this the continued individual existence of the person cannot be inferred. The explanation given is also supported by the fact that the deceased persons appearing in this way are as a rule seen in the clothes they usually wore, and also that a murdered man appears with his murderer, a horse and his rider, and so on.[29]

Schopenhauer also suggests that the 'whole conception of the realm of shades [the spiritual world] probably arose from spirit apparitions'.[30] Schopenhauer resists the inference that apparitions of the dead are caused by the surviving spirits of the dead because his metaphysics commits him to denying that the individual soul survives the death of the body. The phenomenal realm, including the material body, is the realm of individuation. When the individual body perishes, the individual soul perishes as well. The only immortal element of a human being is the will, which is not individual, but common and undifferentiated.

But if the soul does not survive the death of the body, then how does Schopenhauer explain—or explain away—mediumship, in which living people carry on conversations with spirits of the dead? Swedenborg suggests that mediumship is a combination of apparitions of the dead with the imagination of the medium. The medium simply invests the dumb apparitions with imaginary personalities and then carries on conversations with them:

> In all probability, most of the ghosts seen by the clairvoyante of Prevorst are also to be reckoned among visions of this kind [mere images of the dead]. But the conversations she carried on with them are to be regarded as the work of her own imagination that furnished the text for this dumb show from its own resources and thus supplied its explanation. Thus by nature man attempts in some way to explain everything that he sees, or at any rate to introduce some connection and sequence and in fact to turn it over in his mind. Therefore children often carry on a dialogue even with inanimate things. Accordingly, without knowing it, the clairvoyante herself was the prompter of those forms that appeared to her. Here her power of imagination was in the same kind of unconscious activity with which we guide and connect the events in the ordinary insignificant dream, indeed with which we sometimes seize the opportunity for this from objective accidental circumstances, such as a pressure felt in bed, or a sound reaching us from without, an odour and so on, in accordance with which we then dream long stories.[31]

The clairvoyante of Prevorst was Frau Frederica Hauffe, née Wanner (1801-1829), whose exhibitions of clairvoyance and mediumship were related by Justinus Kerner in his celebrated book *Die Seherin von Prevorst* (*The Clairvoyante of Prevorst*).[32] Schopenhauer's library contained an extensively annotated copy of the 1838 third edition of this work, as well as vols. 8-11 of Kerner's *Blätter aus Prevorst* (*Pages from Prevorst*), also annotated, and two other volumes of Kerner's on somnambulism and animal magnetism.[33]

Schopenhauer claims that the fact that a medium's spirit-conversations are often identifiably coloured by the medium's own worldview is evidence in favour of his hypothesis. For instance, he writes of the clairvoyante of Prevorst:

> ...this explanation finds strong confirmation in the unutterable absurdity of the text

of those dialogues and dramas that are alone in keeping with the intellectual outlook of an ignorant girl from the hills and with the popular metaphysics that has been drilled into her. To attribute to them an objective reality is possible only on the assumption of a world order that is so boundlessly absurd and revoltingly stupid that we should have to blush at belonging thereto.[34]

Here Schopenhauer lays his cards on the table, for the 'popular metaphysics' that he finds so 'absurd and revoltingly stupid' that he treats it as a *reductio ad absurdum* of the clairvoyante's revelations is merely the idea that the individual soul survives the death of the body and lives on in a spiritual world. He rejects this metaphysics because it conflicts with his own. He rejects mediumship, because if he took it seriously, it would constitute an empirical refutation of his metaphysical denial of the survival of the individual soul after death.

There are three serious problems with Schopenhauer's argument that mediumship is imaginary because reports of spirits are always coloured by the medium's point of view. First, it proves too much. The same argument can be used to prove that everything is imaginary, because our perception of everything is coloured by our particular points of view. Second, as Schopenhauer himself points out a few pages later in the same essay, the argument is a non-sequitur: 'We often imagine we have abolished the reality of a spirit apparition when we show that it was subjectively conditioned. But what weight can this argument have with the man who knows from Kant's doctrine how large a share the subjective conditions have in the appearance of the corporeal world?'[35] For a Kantian idealist, it simply does not follow that because consciousness is subjectively conditioned, it is not consciousness of something real. Indeed, it is precisely by means of these subjective conditions that we are capable of knowing things at all. Third, not everything in a medium's reports can be reduced to his prior knowledge and point of view. Spirits sometimes report facts otherwise unknown to the medium, facts that can be tested. If these facts can be verified, and if the medium could not have learned of them by conventional means, then we have elegant proof of the veracity of at least some cases of mediumship. Robert Almeder examines a number of such cases in his *Death and Personal Survival: The Evidence for Life After Death*.[36] Schopenhauer himself lists a number of empirically testable reports by the clairvoyante of Prevorst.

> ...if the very prejudiced and gullible Justin Kerner had not secretly had a faint notion of the [imaginary] origin here stated of those spirit conversations, he would not have omitted always and everywhere with such irresponsible levity seriously and zealously to look for the material objects that are made known by the spirits, for example writing materials in church vaults, gold chains in castle vaults, children buried in stables, instead of allowing himself to be deterred from this by the most trifling obstacles. For this would have thrown some light on the facts.[37]

If any of these reports turned out to be true and there were no ordinary way the clairvoyante could have obtained the information, this would prove her veracity. Schopenhauer claims that Kerner did not investigate these claims precisely for fear of refuting the clairvoyante. But we could just as well accuse Schopenhauer of failing to investigate them for fear of proving her right. Such an investigation would not have been difficult for Schopenhauer. He was a man of leisure and independent means. Prevorst was not so far away and the clairvoyante was a younger contemporary who had lived entirely within Schopenhauer's own lifetime.

4. Schopenhauer on Swedenborg

It is important to note that Swedenborg is nowhere mentioned in Schopenhauer's published accounts of paranormal phenomena. His name does, however, appear in Schopenhauer's preliminary notes for his 'Animal Magnetism and Magic' chapter, §106 of his notebook entitled *Adversaria*, which was begun in March of 1828. The ideas expressed in these notes also find their way into the 1851 'Essay on Spirit-Seeing':

> In general it might well be that all dreaming is a function not of the brain, but of the inner nerve-centre, a consciousness of which, however, nothing usually enters the brain as long as this is not yet absorbed in total rest and which then still acts like a spectator; it is therefore *possible* to recall dreams. This possibility, however, would cease if the brain were totally quiescent and the vital force were concentrated entirely

in the ganglionic sensorium, especially if this seized control of the nerves that produce external movement. For this reason those in a deep sleep and especially magnetic as well as natural sleep-talkers and sleep-walkers have, when they are awake, no recollection of the representations or mental pictures of their sleep. Now if we assume this and regard dreams simply as the sensorial activity of the solar plexus which had as its condition the more or less complete exclusion and inactivity of the brain, then the abnormal case could also be conceived where once during wakefulness, and hence while the brain is active, the solar plexus entered a state of sensorial activity whose product, being mixed up with that of cerebral activity, would then suddenly stand out as a *phantom* or *ghost*. This, however, often vanishes when, to observe it more closely, a man focuses his attention on it and hence intensifies the cerebral activity, where at day-break it disappears like a will-o'-the-wisp. Aristotle has already observed that things like this happen…It is highly probable that this is what happens with all *spirit-seeing* and *spirit-hearing*. Now whether such a phenomenon referred to anything objective, that is to say to something different from our own individuality, would depend on whether the sensorial activity of the solar plexus (so abnormally strong that it rises above cerebral activity) had no other cause than a purely physiological one, as for example with Nicolai; or an external cause such as may be the lively thoughts and desires of others, especially of the dying. Whether one who has died can have such an effect is extremely doubtful. The most striking instances of this would be Swedenborg and the clairvoyante of Prevorst…[38]

Schopenhauer also pairs Swedenborg and the clairvoyante of Prevorst in a note on the back end-page of his copy of the French translation *Heaven and Hell* and *Earths in the Universe*:

It appears to have been a spontaneous somnambulism and *clairvoyance*, the memory of which remained in the brain, which however, as with nearly all somnambulists, in whom earlier, and indeed very strong, brain representations were fixed, from which springs the thoroughgoing and decided Christianity of all [his] visions; from which [springs] the polyhistorical thought-tendency of the inhabitants of Mercury, for

Mercury was the God of oratory, and so forth; from which [springs] encounters with Christian von Wolff, Aristotle and many others, who appear according to *Swedenborg's* capacities, and so forth. For though *Swedenborg* was a man of excellent faculties and much knowledge, the visions, since they stood under the influence of the brain, systematically and coherently failed. I would like to say: with such visions the ganglion network supplies *the dumb show*, and the brain speaks the text in addition. So also with the Seeress of Prevorst: She is probably a Seeress, but no Heareress. The same applies to Swedenborg. The spirit world of each of these two therefore corresponds exactly the sphere of their knowledge.[39]

This note requires a bit of unpacking and explanation. First, Schopenhauer thinks that Swedenborg and the clairvoyante had essentially the same sort of visions, namely 'spontaneous somnambulism and clairvoyance'. Spontaneous somnambulism is to be contrasted with induced somnambulism, whether self-induced or induced by another. Somnambulism does not refer to sleep-walking, but to any activity undertaken in a state of trance. In the case of Swedenborg and the clairvoyante, the activity is clairvoyance itself. (Swedenborg also wrote a good deal during his trace states). Second, both Swedenborg and the clairvoyante reported seeing and communicating with the spirits of the dead. Schopenhauer rejects this possibility for reasons given above. Third, Schopenhauer explains away Swedenborg's mediumship the same way he explains away that of the clairvoyante of Prevorst. He even uses the same language. Swedenborg merely saw apparitions of the dead. His imagination endowed the 'dumb show' of these apparitions with personalities, and then he imagined interacting with them. This explains why his accounts of the spiritual world are so obviously conditioned by his own interests and worldview. In spite of his 'excellent faculties and much knowledge', Swedenborg was, in short, calamitously deluded and never caught onto his delusion throughout the decades of his spiritual awakening and the production of dozens of weighty volumes.

Although Schopenhauer links Swedenborg and the clairvoyante of Prevorst, it is significant that she is mentioned in his published work, but Swedenborg is not. This requires an explanation. Schopenhauer thought that Swedenborg and the clairvoyante had essentially the same sort of visions. He also rejected the veracity of their visions for the same reason. Finally, he tried to explain away their visions in essentially the same way. Since Schopenhauer did not think that the clairvoyante's visions were any more veracious that those of Swedenborg, I would suggest that the only reason he does not mention Swedenborg's visions in print is that he thought the clairvoyante's visions were far better documented. Swedenborg, of course, gives extensive first-person accounts of his visions but for the purposes of the scientific study of the paranormal the accounts of other parties are preferred, and Kerner provides voluminous documentation of just this sort.

* * *

Schopenhauer's encounter with Swedenborg has to be described as a missed opportunity. Schopenhauer looked eagerly to natural science and natural history—including the scientific study of paranormal phenomena—because he wished to evaluate his metaphysical system in the light of experience. Naturally, his strongest desire was to see his theorising confirmed, but intellectual honesty also required him to confront evidence to the contrary as well. We need not raise the question of the ultimate veracity of Swedenborg and the clairvoyante of Prevorst in order to question Schopenhauer's handling of their testimonies. Schopenhauer was willing to believe quite a lot of testimony about paranormal phenomena that probably would not be accepted by today's rigorous scientific investigators of the paranormal, much less by axe-grinding materialist debunkers. The testimonies of Swedenborg and the clairvoyante are certainly no less credible than other testimonies accepted by Schopenhauer. Schopenhauer got off to a good start by reading Swedenborg with great care. Yet, in the end, he balked, because if Swedenborg is right, the individual soul survives the death of the body, a possibility that Schopenhauer rejected on metaphysical grounds as 'revoltingly absurd' and 'infamously stupid'.[40] In the final analysis, Schopenhauer was unwilling to question one of his metaphysical tenets. He was, therefore, placed in a very odd position. Although he thought that animal magnetism, somnambulism, clairvoyance, magic, prophecy and apparitions of the dead were real, when it came to mediumship, he joined the ranks of debunkers.

I see Schopenhauer's rejection of Swedenborg as richly ironic. The model of Schopenhauer's 'Essay on Spirit-Seeing' is Kant's *Dreams of a Spirit-Seer*. Not only does

Schopenhauer refer explicitly to *Dreams*, he also mentions it in the most subtle ways, for instance by alluding to its epigraphs.[41] I have argued extensively that Kant was deeply influenced by his encounter with Swedenborg in the early 1760's.[42] In particular, I have argued that two of the very Kantian tenets that Schopenhauer uses to explain the possibility of clairvoyance—the distinction between phenomena and things-in-themselves and the ideal nature of space and time—were so well-suited to that end because they were adopted by Kant from Swedenborg as Kant himself tried to come to grips with clairvoyance.[43] Thus two of the foundational principles of Schopenhauer's theory of the paranormal derive ultimately from Swedenborg, yet in the end Schopenhauer does not see fit even to mention Swedenborg in his published accounts. Another irony is that Schopenhauer's rejection of Swedenborg is ultimately based on a dual rejection of Kant. First, Schopenhauer's inference that the thing-in-itself is a single, undifferentiated will is illegitimate on Kantian grounds. From the Kantian claim that space and time (the principles of individuation) and the principle of causality are the structure of the phenomenal world, we cannot infer that the thing-in-itself is non-spatial, non-temporal, non-individuated and non-causal as Schopenhauer does. Things as they are in themselves could be exactly as they appear to us. We simply do not know. Second, Kant defended the metaphysical possibility that the individual soul survives the death of the body, and he also offered moral arguments for believing that this is so. Schopenhauer's inference that personal survival is impossible is precisely the kind of *a priori* argument of about the way things-in-themselves must be that Kant's critical philosophy shows to be groundless. Perhaps if Schopenhauer had been a better Kantian he would have appreciated Swedenborg more.

Notes

[1] For a list of Schopenhauer's collection of orientalia and his marginalia, see *Der handschriftliche Nachlaß*, vol. 5, *Randschriften zu Büchern*. Arthur Schopenhauer. pp. 319-52. ed. Arthur Hübscher. Frankfurt am Main. Waldemar Kramer, 1968. Henceforth cited as Hübscher 5.

[2] On Schopenhauer's reading and assimilation of Eastern philosophy, see Moira Nicholls, 'The Influences of Eastern Thought on Schopenhauer's Doctrine of the Thing-in-Itself,' in *The Cambridge Companion to Schopenhauer*, ed. Christopher Janaway. Cambridge: Cambridge University Press, 1999.

[3] See the sections on 'Philosophie' and 'Theologie und Religionswissenschaft' in Hübscher 5.

[4] Hübscher 5, 287-91.

[5] Hübscher 5, 287-318.

[6] *Prodromus Philosophiae ratiocinantis de Infinito, et causa finali creationis, deque mechanismo operationis animae et corporis*. E Swedenborg. Dresden and Leipzig. F Hekelii, 1734. In English: *Forerunner of a Reasoned Philosophy Concerning the Infinite and the Final Cause of Creaton also The Mechanism of the Operation of the Soul and the Body*. Translated by J J Garth Wilkinson. London. The Swedenborg Society, 1992. Hübscher 5, 315.

[7] *Les merveilles du ciel et de l'enfer et des terres planétaires et astrals*, par E S[Emanuel Swedenborg], *D'après le témoignage de ses yeux et de ses oreilles*, 2 vols., Translated by A J P Bin. G J Decker, 1782. The two volumes were bound together as one. Hübscher 5, 315.

[8] *De Commercio Animae et Corporis, quod creditus fieri vel per Influxum Physicum, vel per Influxum Spiritualem, vel per Harmonium Praestabilitam*. E Swedenborg. London. 1769. In English: *The Intercourse between the Soul and the Body, which is believed to be either by Physical Influx, or by Spiritual Influx, or by Pre-established Harmony*. Translated by J Whitehead. New York. Swedenborg Foundation,1913.

[9] Hübscher 5, 316.

[10] *Vera Christiana Religio, continens universam Theologiam Novae Ecclesiae, a Domino apud Danielem cap. vii.13, 14, et in Apocalypsi cap. xxi. 1, 2, praedictae*. E Swedenborg. Amstelodami, 1771. In English: *The True Christian Religion, containing the universal theology of the New Church, foretold by the Lord in Daniel 7:13, 14, and in the Revelation 21:1, 2*. Translated by W Dick. London: Swedenborg Society, 1950.

[11] *Der handschriftliche Nachlaß*, vol. 1, *Frühe Manuskripte (1804-1818)*. Arthur Schopenhauer. Edited by Arthur Hübscher. Frankfurt am Main. Waldemar Kramer, 1966. §674, p. 471. Henceforth cited as Hübscher 1. In English: *Manuscript Remains in Four Volumes*, ed. Arthur Hübscher. Translated by E F J Payne, vol. 1, *Early Manuscripts (1804-1818)*. New York. Berg, 1988. §674, p. 521. Henceforth cited as Payne 1.

[12] *Träume eines Geistersehers, erläutert durch Träume der Metaphysik*. Immanuel Kant. 1766. Edited by Rudolf Malter (with supplemental appendices). Stuttgart, Reclam, 1976. In English: *Kant on Swedenborg: Dreams of a Spirit-Seer and Other Writings*. Edited and translated by Gregory R Johnson. West Chester, Pennsylvania. The Swedenborg Foundation, 2002.

[13] Immanuel Kant, Brief an Charlotte von Knobloch, 10 August 1763, in Malter's edition of *Träume eines Geistersehers,* 99-106. In English: To Charlotte von Knobloch, 10 August 1763,

in Immanuel Kant, *Correspondence*, tr. and ed. Arnulf Zweig (Cambridge: Cambridge University Press, 1999), 70-76.

[14] Hübscher 5, 97-98.

[15] *Darstellung des Lebens und Charakters Immanuel Kants von Ludwig Ernst Borowski, von Kant selbst genau revidiert und berichtigt*. Ludwig Ernst Borowski. Königsberg, 1804.

[16] Hübscher 5, 19.

[17] Hübscher 1, §674, p. 471. English trans.: Payne 1, §674, p. 521.

[18] 'Insipid with veracity' was Henry James, Sr.'s customary expression.

[19] *Über die Grundlage der Moral*, in *Sämtliche Werke*, 5 vols. Arthur Schopenhauer. Edited by Wolfgang Freiherr von Löhneysen, vol. 3, *Kleinere Schriften*. Frankfurt am Main. Suhrkamp, 1986. §22, p. 811. In English: *On the Basis of Morality*. Translated by E F J Payne. Indianapolis. Hackett, 1995. §22, p. 213.

[20] Arthur Schopenhauer, 'Nachträge zur Lehre von der Bejahung und Verneinung des Willes zum Leben', in *Sämtliche Werke*, 5 vols., ed. Wolfgang Freiherr von Löhneysen, vol. 5, *Parerga und Paralipomena*, vol. 2. Frankfurt am Main. Suhrkamp, 1986. §165, p. 372. In English, 'Additional Remarks on the Doctrine of the Affirmation and Denial of the Will-to-Live', in *Parerga and Paralipomena*, 2 vols. Translated by E F J Payne. Oxford. Clarendon Press, 1974. vol. 2, §165, p. 315.

[21] Schopenhauer, for example, sometimes uses the term '*Geisterwelt*' (spirit-world) in a manner that calls Swedenborg to mind. See, for example, the end of section §58 of *Die Welt als Wille und Vorstellung*, in *Sämtliche Werke*, 5 vols., ed. Wolfgang Freiherr von Löhneysen, vol. 1. Frankfurt am Main. Suhrkamp, 1986. 443. In English: *The World as Will and Representation*, vol. 1. Translated by E F J Payne. New York. Dover, 1969. 323.

[22] *Über den Willen in der Natur: Eine Erörterung der Bestätigungen, welche die Philosophie des Verfassers seit ihrem Auftreten durch die Empirischen Wissenschaften Erhalten hat*, in *Kleinere Schriften*. Arthur Schopenhauer. In English: *On the Will in Nature: A Discussion of the Corroborations from the Empirical Sciences that the Author's Philosophy has Received Since its First Appearance*. Translated by E F J Payne. New York. Berg, 1992.

[23] Arthur Schopenhauer, 'Versuch über Geistersehn und was damit zusammenhängt', in *Sämtliche Werke*, 5 vols., ed. Wolfgang Freiherr von Löhneysen, vol. 4, *Parerga und Paralipomena*, vol. 1. Frankfurt am Main. Suhrkamp, 1986. 275-372. In English, 'Essay on Spirit-Seeing and Related Phenomena', in *Parerga and Paralipomena*, 2 vols. Translated by E F J Payne. Oxford: Clarendon Press, 1974. vol. 1, 227-309.

[24] 'Essay on Spirit-Seeing', 238-39.

[25] See *Dreams*, part I, ch. 3, 'Anti-Kabbalah—A Fragment of Common Philosophy to Cancel Community with the Spirit-World'. Although this chapter is cast as a reductionistic attempt to 'explain away' apparitions, Kant's account of the mechanism of apparitions is also consistent with them being genuine influxes from a spiritual world. See Gregory R Johnson, 'A Commentary

on Kant's *Dreams of a Spirit-Seer*', Ph.D. Dissertation. Washington, D C. The Catholic University of America, 2001. ch. 8.

[26] 'Essay on Spirit-Seeing', 263.

[27] 'Essay on Spirit-Seeing', 265-66.

[28] 'Essay on Spirit-Seeing', 264.

[29] 'Essay on Spirit-Seeing', 285-86.

[30] 'Essay on Spirit-Seeing', 284.

[31] 'Essay on Spirit-Seeing', 286.

[32] *Die Seherin von Prevorst. Eröffnungen über das innere Leben des Menschen und über das Hereinragen einer Geisterwelt in die unsere*. Justinus Kerner. Stuttgart und Tübingen. J G Cotta, 1829.

[33] Hübscher 5, 302-4.

[34] 'Essay on Spirit-Seeing', 287.

[35] 'Essay on Spirit-Seeing', 298-99.

[36] *Death and Personal Survival: The Evidence for Life After Death*. Robert Almeder. Lanham, Maryland. Rowman and Littlefield, 1992. ch. 5, 'Communications from the Dead'. See also ch. 2, 'Apparitions of the Dead'.

[37] 'Essay on Spirit-Seeing', 287.

[38] Arthur Schopenhauer, *Der handschriftliche Nachlaß*, vol. 3, *Berliner Manuskripte (1818-1830)*, ed. Arthur Hübscher. Frankfurt am Main. Waldemar Kramer, 1970. 528-29. In English: Arthur Schopenhauer, *Manuscript Remains in Four Volumes*. Edited by Arthur Hübscher, translated by E F J Payne, vol. 3, *Berlin Manuscripts (1818-1839)*. New York: Berg. 1989, 575-76.

[39] Hübscher 5, 316. Translation mine.

[40] 'Essay on Spirit-Seeing', 308.

[41] Schopenhauer's epigraph for the essay is from Goethe, but Goethe himself is alluding to a quote from Virgil, *Aeneid*, vi, 268-9 which Kant quotes near the beginning of Dreams, part I, ch. 2. In the closing paragraphs of the 'Essay' Schopenhauer quotes two words, *'aegri somnia'* ('dreams of the sick') from Horace's *Ars Poetica* 7. Kant uses the sentence in which these words occur as the epigraph to the whole of *Dreams*.

[42] See especially my Ph.D. dissertation 'A Commentary on Kant's *Dreams of a Spirit-Seer*' as well as the following articles: 'Kant on Swedenborg in the *Lectures on Metaphysics*: The 1760s-1770s,' *Studia Swedenborgiana* 10, no. 1. October, 1996: 1-38; 'Kant on Swedenborg in the *Lectures on Metaphysics*: The 1780s-1790s', *Studia Swedenborgiana* 10, no. 2. May 1997: 11-39; 'Kant's Early Metaphysics and the Origins of the Critical Philosophy', *Studia Swedenborgiana* 11, no. 2. May 1999: 29-54; 'The Kinship of Kant and Swedenborg', *The New Philosophy* 99, nos. 3 & 4. July-December 1996: 407-23; 'Did Kant Dissemble His Interest in Swedenborg?: The Esotericism Hypothesis', *The New Philosophy* 102, no. 2. July-December

1999: 529-60; and 'Swedenborg's *Positive* Influence on the Development of Kant's Mature Moral Philosophy' in this volume.

[43] See 'A Commentary', Preface and chs. 5 and 7.

Swedenborg and Heavenly Hermeneutics

Lars Bergquist

1.' **M**aster, what shall I do to inherit eternal life?', was the lawyer's question in Luke, chapter 10. Jesus replied, 'What is written in the law? How readest thou?'

The word 'hermeneutics' derives from the Greek verb *hermeneo*, to interpret. In the 1960's and 70's the theory of interpretation, hermeneutics, became increasingly popular, particularly in France, with Paul Ricour, Michel Foucault and Jacques Derrida as leading protagonists. They criticised the simple, romantic idea, that the search for and discovery of the author's meaning, his intention, should be the interpreter's main aim. They argued that there are many meanings present in the text. The naked text is not enough for understanding: we need knowledge of the intertext, that is, we must, while reading, listen to the 'noise of anonymous but yet in a way well known voices in the space around the text'.[1] We must be aware of the fact that texts of all kinds are involved in dialogues with other literary writing. And the reader himself is a participant in the intertextual dialogue.

Within this world-wide discussion of interpretation and meaning, (philosophical rather than philological), Emanuel Swedenborg was seldom mentioned, with one important exception. I refer to the 'Eranos circle', a group of existentially oriented philosophers, theologians, psychologists, linguists and historians who regularly met in Ascona in Switzerland bringing scholars like C G Jung, Henry Corbin, Mircea Eliade, Ernst Benz and Gershom Scholem together. They fully realized that Swedenborg's hermenuetics, his interpretative method, importantly shed some light on the process of reading in general, in Swedenborg's case a reading which is at the same time psychology, theology, theosophy and ontology.

2. Swedenborg's theosophy and theology is based on his reading of the Scriptures. Through what he considered a special divine gift, he claimed the capacity and insight to discern an inner and heavenly meaning to the text. The Bible was always his point of departure. Through its words and meanings he distinguished and formulated hidden *arcana*.

This method of reading, which gave him a prophetic role, is similar to the Christian gnostic's way to knowledge. As the Spanish professor and authority on spiritual hermeneutics José Antonio Antón-Pacheco has underlined, their insight was of a clearly exegetical character. Perhaps the clearest parallel however, is the Shiite and Sufist mysticism and its esoteric interpretation of the Koranic text. I quote Henry Corbin, the great expert on Islamic mysticism:

> The conviction that to everything that is apparent, literal, external, exoteric...there corresponds something hidden, spiritual, internal, esoteric...is the scriptural principle which is the very foundation of Shiism as a religious phenomenon. It is the central postulate of esotericism and of basic importance to esoteric hermeneutics.[2]

And we should not forget Jewish mysticism, where the sacred texts were generally thought to contain secret significations, revealed only to the learned and pious reader. The *Midrasch*, the old Jewish comments to the *Old Testament*, allows for a phenomenological process similar to that of Swedenborg.[3]

3. Swedenborg looked upon the *Old Testament* and the *Gospels*—its letters, words, literal meaning and inner/heavenly sense—as sacred. Such concentration on and attachment to the Bible may be considered from his Lutheran heritage. His father, a bishop, literally

lived every hour of the day with the Scriptures at hand, and knew the Bible by heart. He seems to have incarnated the principle of Lutheran theology by privileging the divine Word, (the Sacraments being only of secondary importance). We might also recall that the *Old Testament* was of historical import not only to Lutheran and Calvinist clergy but also for the secular authorities in the seventeenth and eighteenth centuries as well. It provided an anchor for Evangelic faith, a divine substitute to the rejected Catholic tradition. To these considerations we may add the political importance of the *Old Testament*'s uncompromising emphasis on Divine and human law and order.[4]

4. Swedenborg's religious crisis, described in the *Journal of Dreams* (1743-44), reached its culmination in the notes covering the night between Easter Sunday and Monday, April 6-7, 1744. He shudders and hears a thundering noise 'as if many winds beat together'. A prayer is put in his mouth and his hands are squeezed by another hand:

> ...I continued my prayer, and said, 'Thou hast promised to take to grace all sinners; thou canst nothing else than keep thy word'. At that same moment, I sat in his bosom, and saw him face to face; it was a face of holy mien, and in all it was indescribable, and he smiled so that I believe that his face had indeed been like this when he lived on earth. He spoke to me and asked if I had a clear bill of health. I answered, 'Lord thou knowest better than I'. 'Well do so', said he; that is as I found it in my mind to signify; love me in reality or do what thou hast promised. God give me grace thereto; I found it was not in my power. Wakened, with shudderings.[5]

The Swedenborgian method of theosophic reading and understanding is first hinted at in the *Journal of Dreams* in the entry of October 26-27, 1744. He dreamt about beautiful porcelain vessels which signified to him his future written works. As we know, the vessel or the receptacle for Swedenborg the theosopher, represents the receiving organ for influx from above and its divine knowledge. I quote:

> (I saw)...the whole of that work upon which I am now entering in the name of God; in front, before me, is the part concerning the Worship of God, at the sides the part

concerning the Love; and also that I ought not to take from the wares of others, but my own...May God lead me in the right way!

Swedenborg's famous vision at a London inn occurred about half a year later. According to Carl Robsahm's account he looked upon this event as a turning-point:

From that day I gave up the study of all worldly science, and laboured in spiritual things, according as the Lord has commanded me to write. Afterwards the Lord opened, daily very often, my bodily eyes, so that in the middle of the day I could see into the other world, and in a state of perfect wakefulness converse with angels and spirits.[6]

5. The crisis therefore, ended in a new divine vocation. While writing his *Journal of Dreams* he had, apparently, no clear insight into what this calling really implied: for instance what was meant with a book such as *De Cultu et Amore Dei* [*The Worship and Love of God*]? As we have seen, the sources should have been his own insight and experiences. It was probably only later that he understood that such a vocation involved man's rebirth, or more precisely the conditions of a radical conversion. Only slowly, after systematic studies of the Scriptures—including the editing of enormous indexes and the publication of the fragmentary book about the history of creation with the foreboding title of *The Worship and Love of God*—did he realize that his mission concerned his own rebirth: the radical conversion and call from Christ as recorded in his *Journal*.

From this perspective, it was evident that the fundamental turning point of his own life should be anchored in the Scriptures. Thus, he related his own story to the triadic theme of the Bible: innocence, fall and redemption. In 1745 he began an interpretative analysis of *Genesis* and *Exodus*, which later on, became the nucleus of *Arcana Caelestia* (1747-53). In his voluminous comments on the ancient biblical stories, he discovers that the events described are representations of man's personal regenerative process. Hence, within the *sensus literalis* of the Bible, Swedenborg explored an inner meaning.

Thus, for Swedenborg, the illogical, difficult and incomprehensible was raised to a higher level and given an existential reading. The biblical myths and their heroes became symbols for events or circumstances beyond the visible or quantitatively measurable world, and moved to another qualitative reality.

6. The turning point was epistemological: his knowledge (the insight to which he sought), becomes interiorised. Through dreams, visions, dictates from above, discussions with angels and demons, guided tours in paradise and hell he becomes familiar with what he conceived as the real inner meaning of the Holy Scripture. God is always *'absconditus'*, (hidden), and reveals himself only through his vassals of love, *'i fedeli d'amore'*, the angels and the human beings who are close to them. Angelology becomes insight into the divine, the 'celestial pole' of the mystic's being, where God shows himself and reveals the unknown through angels according to the quest and character of the individual's state of mind.

7. Swedenborg's understanding of the biblical texts are, he says, based on a special permission, a privilege given by God:

...it has pleased the Lord to manifest himself to me, and to send me to teach those things which will be of the new church...For the sake of this end He has opened the interiors of my mind and spirit; by virtue of which it has been granted me to be in the spiritual world with the angels, and at the same time in the natural world with men.[7]

In simple terms, the interpretations given to him are explanations corresponding to the word or meaning being contemplated in the Bible. The angels' speech, he says, is ineffable. He, Swedenborg, can grasp the meaning only if he is in a 'like state' or on the same spiritual level as his interlocutors.[8] His state of mind, even when he is in the spiritual world, is decisive for his understanding. All his movements, his travelling in the other world, is brought about through changes in his mental condition, as explained in the *Arcana Caelestia* §1073. These heavenly alterations of mind correspond to those of the wise man or woman in this world, where divine wisdom corresponds directly to their inner state.

His description of angelic contacts are in this respect similar to what he writes about in *Heaven & Hell* §391 concerning the way angels guard men and draw them away from evil affections. They dwell in our good affections, he says, 'near to man in proportion as he is in good from truths, and more remotely in proportion as the life is distant therefrom'. The difference is that we do not perceive them anymore than we see the demons encouraging our evil inclinations.

8. Angelic knowledge likewise, varies according to state of mind. Swedenborg describes such inner changes in *Heaven and Hell*:

> ...They [angels] have a proprium as well as men, and this consists in loving themselves, and all who are in heaven are withheld from their proprium, and in proportion as they are withheld from it by the Lord, in the same proportion they are in love and wisdom...therefore they have changes of state, or successive vicissitudes...their proprium...continually draws them away.[9]

As their wisdom diminishes so in turn do they become melancholy. 'I have spoken with them when they were in this state, and have seen their sadness', says Swedenborg in §160. 'But they said that they were in the hope of soon returning to their pristine state...for heaven is for them to be withheld from their proprium'.

9. All angelic wisdom is arrived at through the Scriptures, says Swedenborg in *The True Christian Religion* §242. 'The light and wisdom they [angels] enjoy is in the same proportion as the profoundness of their understanding'. And the depth of the insight is in proportion to the character and intensity of their love. The wisdom of the celestial angels is more penetrating than the wisdom of the spiritual angels. The wisdom of the spiritual angels in turn, is superior to that of human beings. Thus, the interpretation of the Word varies according to the state of mind of the angel, and simultaneously therefore influences the spiritual condition of Swedenborg himself, the privileged searcher of the inner sense. From a hermeneutical point of view this implies two layers of meaning, the heavenly and the spiritual. Within these categories of understanding the question of interpretation is more or less clear, and depends upon the interpreter and his listener. The insight into the text becomes an active process, a result of the love and wisdom of the reader.

Is the interpreter an angel therefore, or is it Swedenborg himself? Does the angel incarnate Swedenborg's own state of mind, thus creating an identity between the text, Swedenborg himself and the heavenly messenger? Sebastion Castellio, the translator of a famous Latin version of the Bible which Swedenborg studied daily, wrote in his preface, that 'only the person who has in himself the illumination of the same spirit that gave the original revelation, can see through the garment of the letter to the eternal message, the ever living word within'.

We cannot give a definite answer, but I think we might note that Swedenborg's interpretations never convey abstract notions; they are always concrete, expressing the angel's or Swedenborg's own personal experiences. All is subjective, existentially relevant to the reader; with a personal relation between meaning and interpreter. The biblical text is interiorised, an indication of the readers spiritual maturity.

Thus, Swedenborg's hermeneutics are integral to his anthropological ideas. Man's divine task is to become fully illuminated. Depth of insight is related directly to the strength of will and love and to the readiness to transform knowledge into action. In other words: our earthly mission is to become angels when our short time on earth comes to its end.

10. Angels and spirits: how are we to understand them? Let me make two points:

Firstly, angels are not only manifestations of man's vocation to eternal life, they are also God's face to mankind on earth. 'The angel of His presence saved them', says *Isaiah* (63:9). God, Christ, the Holy Spirit cannot be grasped, the concept is too difficult to fathom for human intelligence. For Christians, God is made visible through the incarnation which shows the way, the truth and the life.

But man feels a need to understand God personally. The *sum qui sum*, 'I am what I am' (*Exodus* 3:14) is not enough. God's concrete manifestation is the *Homo Maximus*, the Grand Man, animated by the divine human; the society of angels in human form, both spiritual and material.

My second point regards the universal character of this concept. Christians of all different varieties as well as Islamic believers have, through time, reckoned with, understood and in their vision seen this primordial form of man. The *Homo Maximus* is, says Corbin, the supreme archetype according to which man was created, the mirror where

God or his angel, the angel who is God's face, has appeared to the visionary in search of religious truth.[10] When Swedenborg in his old age tried to explain his ideas in conversation with visiting countrymen they often took him for an eccentric, weird old man, whose ideas had gone astray, and led him to something close to insanity. There are several reports of this kind and, moreover, we meet this kind of condemnation even today.[11] These statements often seem short sighted and without perspective. Swedenborg's way of thinking is a continuation of a long tradition, where we find the old Christian idea of the Community of the Saints, to the Greek Orthodox concept of Sophia, visions of a long series of Christian mystics, among them Jacob Boehme. And furthermore we meet very similiar concepts in Islamic mysticism. It might have been easier for Swedenborg to explain what he meant if he had been able to put his own thinking into this broader perspective. The core of this tradition considers the integral dimension of man as the meaning of life, and the transformation of the visible into the invisible.

11. The full understanding of Swedenborg's message is also facilitated by seeing him within the context of other existentialist philosophers and theologians. Like Eckhart, Angelus Silesius, Boehme, Pascal, Kierkegaard and Unamuno, Swedenborg's psychology has its point of departure in the notion of man as a potentiality, a demon or an angel placed in a universe of divine meaning. Here, in this meaningful pattern, man has a supreme task, which is to personally engage or be actively involved with the realisation of God's plan for the universe. 'Subjectivity is truth' said Kierkegaard. Our understanding is born through engagement and not by thought processes (such as making deductions from abstract statements of dogma). Swedenborg qualifies this idea by emphasising the idea that man's love, wisdom and activity makes him godlike. His message is an existential humanism say Corbin and Pacheco. Swedenborg's notion of man in a triadic universe (i.e. natural, spiritual and celestial,) is humanistic in the sense that heaven, the church and the angel is man himself. Each individual—through his/her particular profile and character and the full realisation of being human—clarifies and enriches heaven, making it more powerful.

12. Swedenborg's philosophy of meaning is an example of his predilection for thinking

in terms of three connected concepts, or triads. As already mentioned, there is a literal, a spiritual and a celestial sense. These three senses can be analysed in a vertical, successive manner, or in horizontal, simultaneous terms. In both cases, Swedenborg uses the same paradigm: all statements have a final, ultimate aim, a cause, and an effect. He explains his way of thinking in an important passage in *The True Christian Religion*:

> The Word is in its fullness, holiness and power in its literal sense. This is explained by the fact that both the spiritual and the heavenly senses conjoin in the natural, literal sense. The senses' relations to each other can be clarified in the following way:
>
> In successive order one thing succeeds and follows another from the highest down to the lowest; but in simultaneous order one thing stands next to another from inmosts even to outermosts. Successive order is like a column arranged in steps from summit to base, while simultaneous order is like a work coherent with the circumferences from the centre to the outmost surface. I will now explain how successive order becomes simultaneous order in the outmost. The highest things of successive order become the inmost things of simultaneous order, comparatively as a column arranged in steps when it subsides becomes a body coherent in a plane. Thus is the simultaneous formed from the successive, and this in each and all things both of the natural world and of the spiritual world. For there is everywhere a first, a middle and a last, and the first tends and passes through the middle to its last....
>
> Now, in respect to the Word: the celestial, the spiritual and the natural go forth from the Lord in successive order; and in the outmost they exist in simultaneous order. And thus the celestial and spiritual senses of the Word exist simultaneously in its natural sense. When this is comprehended it can be seen how the natural sense of the Word is the containant, the basis and the support of its spiritual and celestial senses; and also how the divine good and truth are in the sense of the letter of the Word in their fullness, their holiness and their power...The celestial and spiritual senses separated from the natural sense are not the Word, for they are like spirit and life without a body...a palace without foundation. [12]

As Henry Corbin wrote in his *God's Face, Man's Face*,[13] Swedenborg here issues a double warning. Firstly, the natural, literal sense will be profaned if the reader forgets its inner sense. Then its sacred character is obliterated. On the other hand, man may corrupt the spiritual or heavenly sense. He then estranges himself from the divine humanity, the true sense in which the angels dwell. Therefore, says Swedenborg in *The True Christian Religion* §208, if 'somebody wants to interpret the spiritual sense of the Word by himself, without the Lord, the heaven becomes closed so that man cannot see the truth, or he is spiritually insane'. It is for this reason, states Swedenborg, that God has posted cherubs to guard the Word in order to prevent man from penetrating into the spiritual meaning and pervert the truth.

13. Swedenborg's divine mission, the revelation of hidden meanings, implies a particular relation to biblical language. An inner sense lies hidden like pearls in the oyster's shell, closed to all living men, with one single exception. I mention this mystical approach to language in order to underline the distance between Swedenborg's method and the more or less rational interpretation of the Bible by way of allegory. Swedenborg's relation to the written word is, as mentioned, phenomenologically similar to the Jewish kabbalists. Both believe in the text as a closed system, containing hidden truths, which are revealed only through divine grace.

14. The guiding, overriding principle in all of Swedenborg's biblical interpretation is religious/moral. This reveals the necessity of the concept of rebirth, which is the very beginning and condition for all theophany. Swedenborg's interpretation of the history of creation (*Genesis*), as described in the first pages of his *Arcana Caelestia,* constitutes the fundament for all his teachings. From this perspective, the first seven days are said to represent the chaotic, earth-bound creature's death and transformation to God's agent and collaborator, bringing about the victory of the empire of love. It is man's *magnum opus,* and Swedenborg was called to be its herald.

During his scientific period Swedenborg had been a metallurgist, and as such a student of alchemy. The list of books in his Stockholm library bears witness of his interest in the *scientia scientiarum*. The classic alchemist's way to gold and truth went through stages which remind us of the mystics' stations or stages on the road to God: *nigredo' putrefactio, dissolutio, coagulum* were both conditions and phases towards the *essentia essentiarum*, the *lapis philosophorum* or *prolectionis*. In human terms; the god-knowing man.

Emanuel Swedenborg, assessor in the Royal College of Mines, was certainly not an adherent of the alchemists' teachings but the phenomenological vicinity of their symbolical languages is well worth studying.

15. Swedenborg, asserting that through a special grace and the endowment of a penetrative and divine clairvoyance, obtained a new way to knowledge. He became aware of hidden correspondences and representations and thus, a divine parallelism between the natural and the spiritual world. He looked upon these correspondences as a new pedagogical instrument, through which he would be able to rationally explain long forgotten truths. The biblical texts have their hidden meanings but not only the Word is representative. Everything in it are tokens or signs of a higher reality. As stated in his *Arcana Caelestia* §2991 and §2993 respectively:

...there is not the least thing in the natural world and in the three kingdoms that does not portray something in the spiritual world, or that does not have something there to which it is responsive...

The same holds true for things in the vegetable kingdom, where there is not the least element that does not portray something in the spiritual world and correspond to it. This I have often been taught by a similar interaction with angels. I have also been told the reasons, namely that the causes of all natural phenomena are from spiritual sources and the fundamentals of those causes from heavenly sources. Or, in other words, everything in the natural world finds its cause in something true that is spiritual, and its fundamental in something good that is heavenly...

16. Swedenborg's method of reading and interpretation renders the meaning of the text dependent on interior movements and changes of consciousness. Interior meaning cannot be found as long as the mind is occupied with outward things.

...heavenly secrets are hidden in the inner sense, and these secrets can only be seen...when the mind ceases to concentrate on the literal meaning. The word of the Lord is like a body in which there is a living soul. The soul does not manifest itself as long as the mind is prisoner of the body. Then the bodily mind can hardly believe that it has a soul, even less that it will live after death. But that which belongs to the soul and to the life appears as soon as the mind leaves the body. This is the reason why not only the bodily must die before man can be reborn, but that also the whole body must die, so that man can come to heaven and see heavenly things...[14]

Swedenborg's teaching of the death of the old man and the consequent birth of the new constitutes, as already mentioned, the spiritual sense behind the particulars of the written word in the Bible. In his hermeneutical circle the whole mirrors the parts, and vice versa. The dogmatic equation is simplified and interiorised.

'It is not the system itself, but the comments that are the legitimate form for approaching the truth', says Gershom Scholem.[15] In the Jewish tradition an omission, an incoherence or lack of clarity in a text is not looked upon as negative but as an opening, a possibility to increase an understanding of the value and richness of the text.

17. 'How readest thou?' This is both a doctrinal and hermeneutical question. Leaving the problems of truth aside it is important that we improve our understanding of Swedenborg's role and teachings. We need a comparative phenomenological approach. Through such a reading we will be better able to distinguish the manner by which Christian mystics and non-Christian theosophers define and solve their problems. We can thus see what unites them and how they differ, and deepen our insight into religious language and the meanings that lie behind it. The most important value of this approach however, is the possibility of arriving at an understanding of Swedenborg's own unique perspective, of the visions, the tensions, the difficulties, contrasts and theophanies that constitute his own spiritual tone and enlightened horizon.

This is a scientific task, but also an ecumenical one (I use the word in its etymological meaning). It is a question of understanding the different voices and ideas of Swedenborg, not simply judging such voices according to reason. We should look to what Kant called *Verstand*, *intellectus*, rather than to the *Vernunft*, *ratio*.

And why ecumenical? Ernst Benz, the German Swedenborg specialist, once said Swedenborg's ecumenical importance lies in the fact that he has reminded us of the real character of language: its capacity to enclose hidden, inner meanings of the words, that they are much more than current coins.

18. A very promising work in this direction has already been done by Henry Corbin, the French specialist in Islamic mysticism, who died in 1978, and his work is continued by professor Jean-Jacques Wunenburger at the University of Dijon and by José Antonio Antón-Pacheco at the University of Sevilla. Important and interesting studies are also made in the Vatican by the Pontificio Institute Orientale: Centro Studi e ricerche Ezio Aletti.

But this is only the beginning of a turning tide. In a letter to his friend Dr Beyer from 1769, Swedenborg complained that there are 'few who admit the understanding into any theological matters...Nor do they allow enlightening themselves in the language of Scripture...'. He spoke of the situation in Sweden 200 years ago, but he could as well have included the whole of the Western world today. Swedenborg was well aware that his teachings would require time before they could become known and understood. But he was very confident. *'Nunc licet entrare in arcane fide'*, he wrote in *The True Christian Religion*. Now it is permitted to enter into the secrets of faith.

Notes

[1] Espmark, Kjell: *Resans formler* 1983, p. 19 et seq and, referred to by Espmark, Beardsley, Monroe: *Aesthetics*, 1958.

[2] *Creative Imagination in the Sufism of Ibn 'Arab*. Routledge & Kegan Paul, London, 1970. p 78: cf also Molla Sadra Shirazi: *Le Livre des penetrations metaphysiques*: Traduit de I'arabe, annote et introduit par Henry Corbin. Collection *Islam Spirituel*. Verdier 1988, p 20 et seq.

[3] Cf José Antonio Antón-Pacheco: *Un libro sobre Swedenborg*. Universidad de Sevilla, 1984. p 53 and, referred to by Pacheco, Brooke, G: 'Qumran Pesher: Towards the Redefinition of a Genre'. *Revue de Qumran* 40, 1981. pp483-505.

[4] Carl-Gustaf Hildebrand: 'Bibel och politik fran 1500- till 1 700-tal' in: *Den svenska bibeln, ett 450-ars jubileum*. Proprius Stockholm, 1991. p 165 et seq.

[5] *Emanuel Swedenborg's Journal of Dreams*. p 22-23. Trans. J J G Wilkinson. 1860. Swedenborg Scientific Association/Swedenborg Society. 1989.

[6] *Documents Concerning Swedenborg*. Editor; R L Tafel. The Swedenborg Society. 1875. Vol 1, doc 5.

[7] *Conjugial Love* §1. E Swedenborg. Trans. J Chadwick. The Swedenborg Society, 1996.

[8] *Apocalpse Revealed* §961. E Swedenborg. The Swedenborg Society, 1970.

[9] *Heaven & Hell* §158. E Swedenborg. The Swedenborg Society, 1958.

[10] *Face de Dieu, Face de l'homme, Flammarion*, Paris, 1983. p 237 et seq.

[11] Lindholm, Lars: Johan Hinric Liden. Lard och resenar. Studier i ide-och lardomshistoria in ActaUniversitatis Upsaliensis. Uppsala 1978, pp 215-216, 272: Kleen, Emil A G: Swedenborg: En lefnadsskildring I-II, Stockholm 1920.

[12] *Arcana Caelestia* §214. E Swedenborg. The Swedenborg Society, 1983.

[13] *Face de Dieu, Face de l'homme, Flammarion*, Paris 1983. See pp. 72-73.

[14] *Arcana Caelestia* §1408. E Swedenborg. The Swedenborg Society, 1984.

[15] *Back to the Source*. Gershom Scholem. p. 14.

[16] *Letters and Memorials of Swedenborg*. Edited by Alfred Acton. The Swedenborg Scientific Association. 1955. p 693.

Representation and Concept in Swedenborg

José Antonio Antón-Pacheco

From the perspective of philosophy, the relationship between thought and literature can be reduced to the relationship between representation and concept. This connects the problem to the question of the origins of philosophy. The dichotomy of representation and concept is a way of expressing the duality of myth and logos.

We have all, no doubt, heard or read about the origins of philosophy as 'the shift from myth to logos'. This is indubitably a superficial vision that does not stand up to examination. But what then do we mean by myth and logos? The logos is a concept that always brings us to the thought of the intelligible. Logos means the essential determinacy of each thing, its reason and intelligibility. In the discourse of the logos, the discourse of concept and unifier will always predominate.

Myth, however, has a sense of history, narrative, story, poem. The verb *mythéomai* means, among many other things, to tell a story. Originally, neither the term myth nor the verb from which it comes had the meaning of legend or chimera that we usually give it today. Myth is fundamentally characterised as a narration, that is, as a story told with images and representations. Within this same order of things, we can establish a similar difference between the *halajà,* or normative and judicial interpretation in Jewish exegesis, and *hagadà* or narrative interpretation (the verb *nagad* also means to tell a story). Myth and logos here are not opposed but are two kinds of discourse, or exposition of ideas. Mythical discourse is characterised by being narrative and representative (it can be imagined) whilst logos is characterised as being conceptual and unified (its ideal is the mathematical demonstration).

It becomes obvious from this, that the origins of philosophy cannot be set in this supposed distinction between myth and logos. In fact it is exactly the opposite. Throughout the history of philosophy—from the Greeks—we can see how the same thinker alternates narrative discourse with elements that are conceptual or purely intellectual. This is the case with Plato for whom myth serves to access places that the concept cannot reach. Plato's myths express what the logos finds ineffable. In the case of Plato therefore, we find no contradiction between myth and logos (and who can have doubts about his rationality?). Myth simply goes further than logos, it reaches more profound depths of being and consciousness than the concept. In fact myth is already logos in so far as it introduces determinacy and organises reality by unifying and presenting it in a coherent manner.

Of course, Plato is not the only one. Throughout the history of ideas we see philosophers rooted in conceptual thought resorting to the use of narrative and representation in order to express their reflections more faithfully (or in a narrative discourse better suited to the kind of cognitive experience that they wish to express). Alongside their rigorously conceptual expositions for instance, Avicenna or Sohravardi wrote narratives in which the transcendental order is made vivid as an initiation adventure. This is expressed in the *falsafa-hikmat* dichotomy. The poem of Parmenides (also a visionary tale) combines, with little concern for continuity, representative figures with ontological statements. Philo of Alexandria explicitly introduces narrative as an object of philosophical analysis. In the same way *Don Quixote and Sancho* in Unamuno or *Abraham and Don Juan* in Kierkegaard also tell us of the vicissitudes of the logos. They are myths in the strictest sense of the word (i.e. they do not determine the logos but shape and channel it into complex meanings).

It is not only the concept or categories of philosophy however that are expressed in this representative language. Any deed or experience that has a particularly relevant or profound meaning, that radically affects the essence of the human being, tends to be ordered in this way. More precisely, it might be said such experiences are narrated in order to acquire a constitutive form. Mystical experiences are a particular example of this. The mystical experience of the ineffable needs a symbol in order to express the experience itself. Such symbols or metaphors subsequently become the privileged language of narration and in fact make up the very fabric of visionary and initiation narratives. We can deduce from this a certain pre-eminence of representative language over conceptual language, of the symbol over the logos. This is why René Guénon, unlike Hegel, believed that a philosophy set in symbolic moulds (for him the Vedas and Indian thought in general) got closer to the essence of the real, than a philosophy which unfolds within the limits of the concept. Myth is pluralistic and has a variety of dimensions. Narrative forms offer constants and archetypes for the sensory. For example, *The Epic of Gilgamesh* (possibly humanity's oldest book) contains paradigms that will then be repeated in real history. Narrative myth repeats a fundamental event that in itself, in the movement of repetition, makes this event present. In short, both ontological paucity and mystical ineffability need narrativisation in order to determine accessible, repeatable and communicable expression.

To return: the order of concepts *versus* the order of images. We may understand this to mean the order of concepts *up to* the order of images, since the concept needs the image to fulfil its own essence. The two orders are not contradictory, but complementary. Maybe, and because of this, poetry is at the very origin of philosophy (Parmenides, Rig Veda X, 129, *Book of Tao*).

We shall now see if what we have said about the relationship between narrative discourse and conceptual discourse is applicable to the case of Emanuel Swedenborg (Stockholm, 1688—London, 1772). There are two aspects of this: the first concerns Swedenborg's work, and the second concerns the projection of the Swedish visionary onto posterity.

In the first instance, we need to begin with the circumstances from which Swedenborg's visionary and theological works are seen to emerge. After the existential crisis in 1743-44 Swedenborg abandoned his scientific work (which started with mathematics and moved towards anatomy) and decided to systemise his spiritual or mystical experiences. He left a large output of scientific works, the most important of which are: *The Principia or First*

Principles of Natural Things [*Principium Rerum Naturalium,* 1743], *The Infinite and Final Cause of Creation* [*Prodromus de Infinito,* 1734], *The Cerebrum* [*De Cerebro,* 1738], *The Economy of the Animal Kingdom* [*Oeconomia Regni Animalis,* 1740-2], *The Animal kingdom* [*Regnum Animale,* 1744-45], etc. During this period, dominated by the scientific thought of Aristotle, Descartes and Wolff among others, Swedenborg shows his interest in spiritual issues (i.e. on the relationship of the body and soul, of God and the world, of faith and works, etc.). He realised that science, enlightened rationalism and Lutheran theology are unable to solve the problems presented here. This culminated in a deep crisis recognised in the book the *Journal of Dreams* [*Drömboken*]. His theological work (which consists of setting out his visions in an ordered fashion) begins at this point and occupies the rest of his life: *Arcana Caelestia* (1749-56), *The Last Judgment* [*De Ultimo Judicio,* 1758], *Apocalyspe Revealed* [*Apocalypsis Revelata,* 1766], *Conjugial Love* [*De Amore Conjugalis,* 1768], *The True Christian Religion* [*Vera Christiana Religio,* 1771] and many other works, some of which were published posthumously. Now is not the time however, to discuss the actual contents of Swedenborg's visionary experiences, nor his theological systemisation. What we shall attempt to stress is the manner by which he expressed and communicated those contents.

Significantly enough, figurative elements start to appear in Swedenborg's work during this stage (i.e. which we might characterise by its transcendental mystical experiences) that gave rise to the later theological work. In fact, here we really need to talk unequivocally about an intermediate phase in the work of the Swedish philosopher that mediates between the scientific and the theological phases. This phase can be seen to continue the problems and categories of the scientific work but at the same time transforms them. This is where his representative language develops in direct relation to his internal experiences. This intermediate phase begins with the *Journal of Dreams* [*Drömbok*]—which collects the visions of 1744, published in Stockholm in 1859—but is above all reflected in his *The Spiritual Diary* [*Experientiae Spirituales,* 1745-1765] where Swedenborg records his narratives in preparation for later publications. *The Worship and Love of God* [*De Cultu et Amore Dei*], which was started before the *Journal of Dreams* but published in London in 1745 stands apart from this. *The Worship and Love of God*[1] is the culmination of the scientific phase, but at the same time recognises its limits. This is shown in the very structure and language of the book. On the one hand *The Worship and Love of God* collects the physical and biological theories given in the *Principia, The Infinite* and *The Economy of the Animal Kingdom*, and on the other it includes a poetic and rhetorical language full of images and allegories. The fact that the work is unfinished shows that the problems it addresses are unsolvable or at least in conflict. The metaphysical and theological problems affecting the author cannot be answered with conceptual language. The new phase requires a transformation of language to the extent that consciousness itself is transformed. The need for another kind of language is being announced, the language of the concept against the language of the image.

As we have said many times, an essential peculiarity of Swedenborg is that the representation process is carried out as the exegetic process develops. Explanations, experiences and representations can be seen to form a unitary movement. After all, biblical interpretation consists in explaining representations. This is again seen in *The Worship and Love of God* (which is really a *Hexameron*) and *The Spiritual Diary*, which are ultimately instances of biblical hermeneutics. This intermediate phase of Swedenborg sees both rationalist and scientific discourses exhausted, it prepares the suppositions that are developed in the theological phase and marks the beginning of the mystical experiences. As such, the emergence of narrative discourse coincides with the appearance of visionary experience. This is the motive for Swedenborg's writings: to show the developments of the inner life in narrative fashion, and for this he has to use the symbol as a privileged vehicle to express spiritual realities. Moreover, someone who has come in contact with the Absolute changes his language, the mundane and everyday is no longer of use to him. For this reason the words of Jürgen Baden are very appropriate:

> A man has been reached by the ray of faith. From this time his life is split in two, he will speak of an old and a new life. Both forms of life are so irreparably separate that the continuity of destiny and of name is only a formality. The converted man perceives that a huge abyss has opened between the present and the past, between now and then. He does not understand his former life and knows that he can never go back. The conversion has revealed a new dimension in his destiny. In this way a total change is made in the evaluation of people, things and events.[2]

Thus the new existential horizon requires a new language to express it.

After this intermediate stage Swedenborg is forced to represent the concept, he has to narrativise it, express it and outline it into images. The hermeneutic key to understand this aspect of Swedenborg's work lies in the word *representation* [*repraesentatio*]. Not only are natural realities representations of spiritual or celestial realities, but these are themselves representations (or at least they have to be represented in order to be understood). From this it follows that the representations of the spiritual world have an ontological weight with regard to fantasies and the imagination [*phantasiae, imaginationes*] which are characterised as having a phantasmagorical reality.[3] As such, representations constitute the metaphysics of the real (and we could say, the ontology of the good, the essence and the figures of positivity), whilst fantasies on the other hand, constitute the metaphysics of deliquescent entities (the first of which is the inessential, the ontology of the bad and obscure, or the forms of negativity). It is not just a question of saying that Swedenborg's language is representative but that his very ontology becomes an ontology of image and representation. It could be said that Swedenborg's scientific phase (with all its problems) necessitated this aspect of figurative schematisation in order to acquire its fullness and resolution.

We now need to apply what we have said. Swedenborg's work needs figurative narration as the form of its finality. This in turn, is complemented by the use of concepts corresponding to the scientific phase: the order of the concepts versus the order of images.

The movements and flow of consciousness described in Swedenborg's spiritual adventures therefore, are determined by images and configurations (i.e. of angels, qualitative time and space, spiritual body, distances and subtle geographies etc.). In the same way (and consequently) such images and configurations are made concrete by narrative discourse. Swedenborg's theological concepts are represented as figures not because the figures are allegories of the concepts but because they are really experienced as figures and concrete entities, both individual and personal. Swedenborg has to express his experiences in a representative discourse because such experiences are representative and not subsumed by the concept. In short, the use of narrative offers a model that both structures and supports the movements of the inner world. For this reason a familiarity with Swedenborg's literary expression or style is essential for a correct understanding of his religious oeuvre.[4] The narrative structures of the written works are identical to the experience of his thought. As we said above, Swedenborg's ontology is essentially an ontology of representation and image (*mundus imaginalis, alam al-mizal*, to use the formulae that Henry Corbin is so fond of).

Starting from his work *Apocalypse Revealed* (1766) Swedenborg introduces a descriptive variation to his visionary experiences. We are referring to the *Memorabilia* [*Memories* or *Memorable Stories*]. These are the vivid narratives which the author introduces after the theological arguments which are divided into chapters. The *Memorabilia* are notable for their literary style and expressive elaboration of narrative. For instance, the *Recuerdos* [Memories] that appear in *Conjugial Love* have a special tone and the question of style is more evident (that is, its literary character). Finally, some of these visionary narratives appear again as additions to *The True Christian Religion* (the situation or representation in the spiritual world of Luther, Melanchton, Calvino, the Dutch, German, Catholics, Africans, Muslims, Jews, etc.). Swedenborg's tendency to turn any idea or concept into an image is clearly seen. It is as if Swedenborg is reminding us that mythical and poetic imagery is needed in order to build a coherent religious vision: concepts are not enough. In summary, there is a correlation between spiritual experience, ontology and language which explains the use of narrative in Swedenborg.

The second aspect worthy of attention here, as mentioned earlier, concerns the influence that the Scandinavian visionary has had on posterity. In this, we mean his influence on writers, poets and artists. It is worth reflecting on the fascination held by poets and writers in general for Swedenborg. Initially, it might appear an exaggeration to say that there is no understanding of Romanticism without an understanding of Swedenborg but if we look at the list of authors who have come under his influence in one way or another, this affirmation becomes very plausible: Novalis, Heine, Blake, Coleridge, Balzac, Almqvist, Emerson, Jung-Stilling, Flaxman, Carlyle, Gerard de Nerval, etc. To all these we need to add Baudelaire and literary symbolism (to the point that Octavio Paz makes Swedenborg the creator of modern poetry), and the list of names gets larger to include Dostoyevsky, Jorge Luis Borges, Unamuno, Ekelöf, Ekelund, Strindberg, Eugenio D'Ors, Arnold Schönberg,

Czeslaw Milosz, etc. All this before we even consider the influence that Swedenborg had on the philosophers Oetinger, Schelling and Krause, and the theologians of the Church of the New Jerusalem (a faith created by some of Swedenborg's disciples after his death).

We might say that the reason for this interest, is that the poet sees in Emanuel Swedenborg someone who tells of his experiences of the transcendental in images and concrete forms and not in the abstract and conceptual language of categories (*philosophemes* or *theologemes*). Swedenborg is a thinker for whom narration is more important than concept, and determinacy is more important than abstract identity. It is natural that the poet should be more inclined to reflect his theological and metaphysical ideas figuratively rather than through the vehicle of a range of categories. The poet even prefers representation when he wants to make up a system of ideas. This is what happened with Romanticism. For the great Swedish poet Carl Jonas Love Almqvist, Swedenborg brought to Romanticism the intellectual programme that it lacked and so corrected the fault of not having any concretisation. But this programme was elaborated not just with theological or philosophical ideas, but with images and figures as well. We find narrative discourse alongside the logos in Swedenborg. In my opinion this is why Swedenborg influenced a large number of writers, especially the Romantics. We will not go into the question of whether the Romantic understanding of Swedenborg's work was correct or not. Swedenborg's narrative inspired the narrative of a large number of writers and artists regardless, and not just as a literary motif (what Karl-Erik Sjöden called 'literary Swedenborgism')[5] but also, fundamentally, as a determinant model and realiser of ideas and experiences that would have been otherwise diluted, either in the world of pure concept or pure indeterminacy.

Swedenborg sets out suppositions which are religious, metaphysical, existential and mystical. But he does not just do this with a system (the logos). He puts all these suppositions into a construction that is narrated, has images and is represented (myth). The poet captures the former with the latter and in the latter.

But Swedenborg's presence among poets is not a thing of the past, it still goes on. Miguel Florián is both a philosopher and poet (with several books of poetry to his credit) and therefore has two reasons for the Northern Prophet to be present in his work. I would like to mention one of his poems titled *Swedenborg*, that belongs to the book *Anteo*[6] [*Antaeus*]. He says:

Representation and Concept in Swedenborg

A sus labios descendian los ángeles
con sus alas de plata, le obsequiaban
con palabras de eternidad,
maravillosos fuegos, armonías
de planetas, de músicas, de hogueras.
En las calles de Londres, el murmullo
del viento anunciaba la escarcha
de sus cuerpos, los ángeles más blancos
le traían recuerdos de otra vida,
como a esos ancianos—tan secretos—
que recogen la luz del mediodía.

[Angels descend to his lips
with silver wings they praise
with words of eternity,
wonderful fires, harmonies
of planets, music, bonfires.
In the streets of London the murmur
of the wind announced the frost
of its bodies, the whitest angels
brought him memories of another life
like to those so secret ancients
who gather the light of melody.]

This poem has obvious echoes of Jorge Luis Borges' excellent sonnet[7] about Swedenborg.

Más alto que los otros, caminaba
Aquel hombre lejano entre los hombres (...)

[He walked higher than the others
That man, far off among men (...).]

Certainly, no Borges 'specialist' seems to have realised this recurrence of Swedenborg throughout Borges' works.[8] I believe that Swedenborg's ideas and experiences figure in the horizon of the Argentinian's metaphysical and religious perspectives. But to return to Miguel Florián. I believe that the inspiration for his poem is more literary than anything else. That is to say one receives the impression that it is not philosophical or theological themes that underlie Miguel Florián's work. The name of Swedenborg, his air of legend and mystery that always surrounds him is the real inspiration of this beautiful poetic text. Apart from the angels there is no direct reference in the poem to the fundamental and characteristic themes of Swedenborg's works. As we have said earlier we are in the presence of what Sjöden called literary Swedenborgism—which does not imply a lack of sincerity in the literary act itself.

We shall now briefly introduce another writer who has also used Swedenborg for the theme of a poem. This is Carlos Liscano and his book *Miscellenea Observata* [Miscellaneous Observations].[9]

Emanuel Swedenborg era un hombre de sistema.
En su casa Hornsgatan, en el centro de Estocolmo,
Emanuel hablaba con los ángeles.
Para dilucidar una idea se reunió con Leibniz en el Cielo
veinte años después de la muerte de Leibniz.
Swedenborg tenía razón.

(Tercos pájaros de invierno
cantan en el bosque muerto.)

[Emanuel Swedenborg was a man of systems.
In his house in Hornsgatan, in the centre of Stockholm,
Emanuel spoke with the angels
To clarify an idea he met with Leibniz in the Heavens
Twenty years after Leibniz' death.
Swedenborg was right.

(Stubborn winter parrots
sing in the dead wood)]

Is Liscano's use of Swedenborg just a literary device here? As in other cases, an explanation based on formalistic literary considerations is not enough. The poems of Miguel Florián, Carlos Liscano or Borges himself do not contain an explicit declaration of Swedenborgism, but pulsate and resound with intangible transcendental and metaphysical yearnings. In other words there is something in these writings that can only be expressed by narrative discourse, or what amounts to the same thing, by myth.

Notes

[1] Cf. *Swedenborgs skapeldrama de cultu et amore Dei.* Inge Jonson. Stockholm, 1961; *Swedenborgs hemlighet. Om ordets betydelse, änglarnas liv och tjänsien hos Gud.* Lars Bergquist. Stockholm, 1999; *Emanuel Swedenborg: El habitante de dos mundos. Obra científica, religiosa y visionaria,* [The inhabitant of Two Worlds. Scientific, Religious and Visionary Work]. Christen A Blomm-Dahl and J A Antón-Pacheco, Eds. Madrid, 2000.

[2] *Literatura y conversión*, [Literature and Conversion]. H Jürgen Baden. p. 11. Madrid, 1969.

[3] There is a great phenomenological similarity between Swedenborg's and Sohravardi's figurative visions. In effect Swedenborg's notion of fantasy approximates to Sohravardi's notion of *barzac*, that is the limit that separates the light from the darkness inherent in contingent beings. For Swedenborg as well, the main characteristic of the deliquescent or fantastic realities is darkness compared with the luminosity identified with representations. On the other hand Sohravardi is also a philosopher who combines conceptual thought with narrative. Cf. Shihaboddin Yahya Sohravardi, *L'Archange empourpré. Qunze traités mystiques de Sohravardi* [The Crimson Archangel. Fifteen Mystical Treatises of Sohravardi] translated from the Persian and Arabic by Henry Corbin, 1976: *Le livre de la sagesse oriental* [*The Book of Oriental Wisdom*] (Kitab Hikmat al-Ishraq), *Commentaire de Qotboddin Shirazi et Molla Sadra Shirazi, traduction et notes par Henry Corbin, établies et introduites par Christiann Jambet, Lagrasse,* 1986 [Commentaries by Qotboddin Shirazi and Molla Sadra Shirazi, edited and introduced by Christiann Jambet]. Swedenborg would by antonomasia be a philosopher of the *mundus imaginalis* or transcendental imagination, hence the representative character of his discourse.

[4] In having this need for image and scheme in elaborating his philosophical discourse, Swedenborg shows great similarities with the Spanish philosopher Eugenio D'Ors (1881-1954), who at the time wrote some very intelligent notes on the Prophet of the North *in Introducción a la vida angélica* (2nd edition) [*Introduction to the Angelic Life*], Madrid, 1987. Cf my article *Presencia de Swedenborg in Eugenio D'Ors*, [*Swedenborg's Presence in Eugenio d'Ors*] in *Un libro sobre Swedenborg*, [*A Book on Swedenborg*], Seville University, 1999 (translation into English by Robert E. Shillenn as *Visionary Consciousness. Emanuel Swedenborg and the Immanence of Spiritual Reality*, Charleston, 2000).

[5] *Swedenborg en France*, [*Swedenborg in France*]. Karl-Erik Sjöden. Stockholm, 1985.

[6] *Anteo*. Miguel Florián. Huelva, 1994.

[7] *El otro, el mismo* [*The Other, the Same*] in *Obra poetica* [Poetic Work]. Jorge Luis Borges. Madrid 1972.

[8] I discussed Borges' Swedenborgism in *La religiosidad de Jorge Luis Borges, a propósito de Swedenborg*, [*The Religiousness of Jorge Luis Borges, with Reference to Swedenborg*] op cit. and later in *El centenario del nacimento de Jorge Luis Borges* [*The Centenary of the Birth of Jorge Luis Borges*] *Letra y Espíritu*, no. 6, 1999.

[9] *Miscellanea observata*. Carlos Liscano. Montevideo, 1995. The attentive reader will appreciate that this is also the title of one of Swedenborg's works.

Index

Abraham and Don Juan 112
Act of Creation 59
Additional Remarks on the Doctrine of the Affirmation of the Will-to-Live 80
Adversaria 88
Agrippa, Henricus Cornelius 77
Alcibiades 67
Almeder, Robert 87
Almqvist, C J L 117, 118
Alphonso 26
Anatomi af wår aldrafinaste natur 41
Animal Kingdom, The 114
Animal Magnetism and Magic 81, 88
Anteo [*Antaeus*] 118
Apocalypse Revealed 114, 117
Apocalypsis Revelata 114
Apollinaris the Yonger 71
Apostles Creed 71
Aquinas, Thomas 60, 63
Arcana Caelestia xiv, 1, 3, 9, 60, 62, 63, 65, 66, 68, 70, 71, 72, 79, 100, 101, 106, 107, 114

Archiv für den Thierischen Magnetismus (*Archive of Animal Magnetism*) 77
Aristotle 52, 59, 60, 63, 70, 71, 78, 89, 90, 114
Athanasius 71
Avicenna 71, 72, 112

Baader, Franz von 77
Baden, J 115
Balzac, H de 117
Baudelaire, C 117
Benz, Ernst 98, 109
Benzelius, Eric 41, 45
Berkeley, George 62, 64
Beyer, Dr 109
Bible, The 98, 99, 100, 101, 103, 106, 108
Biran, Maine de 72
Blake, William 117
Blätter aus Prevorst (*Pages from Prevorst*) 86
Boehme, Jacob 77, 104
Book of Tao 113
Borges, Jorge Luis 119, 120, 121

Borowski, Ludwig Ernst 79
Boyle, Robert 61
Broad, C D 61
Bruno, Giordano 77
Buddhism 64, 68, 77

Campanella, Tomasso 77
Carazan's Dream 24, 25
Carlyle, T 117
Cartesian 6, 41, 49, 69
Castellio, Sebastion 103
Cerebrum, The 114
Coleridge, S T 117
Conjugial Love 114, 117
Copernicus 22
Corbin, Henry 98 103, 104, 105, 109, 117
1 Corinthians 70, 71
Cottrell, A 70
Crasta, Francesca Maria 62
Critical Philosophy xiv
Critique of Practical Reason 34
Critique of Pure Reason 13, 33
Crusius 21
Cusa, Nicholas of 77

D'Ors, Eugenio 117
Darstellung des Lebens und Charakters Immanuel Kants 79
De Amore Conjugiali 114
De Anima 51
De Cerebro 114
De Commercio Animae et Corporis 40, 52, 78
De Cultu et Amore Dei 100
De Mechanismo Animae et Corporis 42
De Ultimo Judicio 114
Death and Personal Survival: The Evidence for Life After Death 87
Descartes, René 52, 60, 62, 64, 66, 69, 114
Democritus 61, 62, 63, 64
Derrida, Jacques 97
Die Seherin von Prevorst (The Clairvoyante of Prevorst) 86
Don Juan and Sancho 112

Dostoyevsky, F 117
Dreams of a Spirit-Seer, as Elucidated Through Dreams of a Metaphysician xiii, xv, 1-20, 21, 30, 33, 79, 83, 91, 92

Earths in the Universe 78, 89
Eckarthausen, Karl von 77
Eckhart, Meister 77, 104
Economy of the Animal Kingdom 40, 50, 114, 115
Ecstatic Journey of an Enthusiast Through the Spirit World 79
Edinburgh researchers 64, 65
Egyptian Dialogue 69
Ekelöf, 117
Ekelund, 117
Eliade, Mircea 98
Emerson, R W xiii, 117
Emile 28
Epic of Gilgamesh, The 113
Epicurian 6
Eranos Circle 97
Essay on Spirit-Seeing and Related Phenomena 81, 88, 91
Essay on the Sicknesses of the Head 23
Exodus, Book of 100, 103
Experientiae Spirituales 114
Eysenck, H J 70

Ficino, Marsilio 77
Flaxman, John 117
Florián, Miguel 118, 120, 121
Foucault, Michel 97
Freud, Sigmund 72

Gabriel 71
Galileo 61
Genesis, Book of 100, 106
God's Face, Man's Face 105
Golconda 25
Gospels, The 98
Gregory of Nyssa 71
Groundwork of the Metaphysics of Morals 28

Index

Guardian, The 62
Guénon, René 113

Hamilton, William 67, 72
Hamlet 80
Hartmann, Eduard von 72
Hauffe, Frau Frederica née Wanner 86
Heaven and Hell 78, 79, 89, 101, 102
Hegel, G W F 113
Heine 117
Herbart, J F 72
Hercules 69
Hinduism 77
History and Natural Description of the Most Remarkable Occurrences Associated with the Earthquake... 22
Hobbes, Thomas 61
Horatio 80
Hübscher, Arthur 77
Hume, David 21, 28, 60, 67
Hutcheson, Francis 21, 28

Inaugural Dissertation 12, 14
Infinite and Final Cause, The 45, 78, 114, 115
Interaction of the Soul and Body, The 40, 52, 78
Isaiah, Book of 103
Islamic mysticism 98, 104, 109

James, The book of 68
James Sr, Henry 80
Jaspers, Karl xiv
Jesus Christ 71, 97
Journal of Dreams 99, 100, 114
Judges, Book of 69
Jung, C G 72, 98
Jung-Stilling, Johann Heinrich 77, 117

Kant, Immanuel xiii, xiv, xv, 1-20, 21-38, 68, 79, 82, 83, 87, 91, 92, 108
Kantian 82, 87, 92
Kantianism 21
Kerner, Justinus 86, 88, 91

Kierkegaard, Soren 104, 112
Knobloch, Charlotte von 79
Koestler, A 59
Koran 71
Koranic Text 98
Krause 118

Last Judgment, The 114
Laywine, Alison 5
Leade, Jane 77
Lectures on Metaphysics (Hamilton) 67
Lectures on Metaphysics (Kant) 11, 15
Leibniz, G W xvi, 21, 49, 52, 63, 64, 72, 120
Leibnizian 6
Liscano, Carlos 120, 121
Locke, J 60, 61, 62, 64, 67, 68
Luke, Gospel of 97
Lull, Ramon 77
Luther 117

Mechanism of the Soul and Body 42
Mendelssohn, Moses 2, 3, 4, 8
Midrasch 98
Milosz, C 118
Mirandola, Giovanni Pico della 77
Miscellaneous Observations 120
Miscellenea Observata 120
Mohammed 71
Mulla Sadra 72
Myers, F W H 72

neo-Kantian 82
Nerval, G de 117
New Philosophy, The xiii
Newton, Isaac 26, 61, 62
Newtonian 26, 32
Nietzschian xv
Novalis 117

Observations on the Feeling of the Beautiful and the Sublime 23, 24
Odyssey 66
Oeconomia Regni Animalis 40, 50, 114
Oetinger 118

Old Testament 98, 99
On the Basis of Morality 80
On the Will in Nature 81
On Tremulation 41
Opera Philosophica et Mineralia 40
Opusculum 78
Oxford Dictionary of Mythology 70
Oxford Latin Dictionary 66

Pacheco, J A A 98, 104, 109
Paracelsus 77
Parerga and Paraliomena 80
Parmenides 112, 113
Pascal, Blaise 104
Paul 70
Paz, Octavio 117
Philo of Alexandria 112
Plato 59, 70, 112
Platonic 3, 6, 59, 67
Pope, A 21, 26
Pordage, John 77
Post-modern xiv
Post-structuralist xiv
Prince, M 61, 69
Principia, The 40, 44, 45, 47, 49, 113-14, 115
Principium Reurm Naturalium 114
Principles of Philosophy, The 66
Prodromus de Infinito 45, 78, 114
Psychologia Empirica 48, 49, 50
Psychologia Rationalis 50

Rational Psychology 51, 60, 62, 65, 66, 71
Reid, Thomas 61
Regnum Animale 114
Remarks 23, 25, 26, 29
Republic, The 70
Ricour, Paul 97
Robsahm, Carl 100
Romans, The Book of 70
Romanticism 117, 118
Rousseau 21, 23, 25, 26, 27, 28, 29, 31, 33

Rousseauian 25, 26, 27, 29, 32, 33

Saladin 72
Sargent 70
Schelling, F W J xiii, 118
Scholem, Gershom 98, 108
Schönberg, A 117
Schopenhauer, A xvi, 77-95
Shaftesbury 21, 28
Shah Wali Allah 72
Shell, Susan 29
Shi'ite 98
Silesius, Angelus 77, 104
Sjöden, Karl-Erik 118, 120
Sohravardi 72, 112
Spiritual Diary, The 114, 115
Strindberg, A 117
Study of Instinct, The 59
Sublime 11

Tauler, Johannes 77
1 Thessalonians 71
Timaeus 70
Tinbergen, N 59
True Christian Religion, The 68, 78, 79, 80, 102, 105, 106, 109, 114, 117
Tylor, E B 69

Unamuno 104, 112, 117
Universal Natural History and Theory of the Heavens 22, 23, 24, 29

Vera Christiana Religio 78, 79, 114
Vulgate, The 70

Wolff, Christian von xvi, 21, 48, 49, 50, 51, 78, 90, 114
Word Explained, The 70
Worship and Love of God, The 100, 114, 115
Wunenburger, Jean-Jacques 109

Zoroastrianism 72